AF728934

SMALL-BATCH BREADS

REBECCA EISENBERG

Photographs by Linda Campos

SMALL-BATCH BREADS

50 Recipes for Loaves, Buns, and Flatbreads

MADE WITH 1 CUP OF FLOUR

TEN SPEED PRESS
California | New York

CONTENTS

INTRODUCTION

Hi, hello! Do you want to make bread but keep finding recipes that produce giant loaves? Or worse, *multiple* giant loaves of bread you know will go bad before you can finish them? Maybe you live alone, have a small family, or are an empty nester who used to make bread for your large family but aren't sure how to do it now that your kids are out of the house. Maybe you have a small kitchen and find it baffling how so many bread recipes expect you to manage large quantities of dough on a tiny kitchen counter. Or maybe you're frugal and don't want to use up half a bag of flour to make more bread than your freezer can handle. I hear you. I got you.

Small-batch breads to the rescue.

I started making small-batch breads during the early days of the pandemic lockdown as a way to save money on ingredients during recipe testing, intending to scale up the recipes to full-size in the end. I had only recently started my blog, *The Practical Kitchen*. I hadn't yet gone to pastry school, and though I had been a hobby baker for almost a decade, I was new to recipe development. Scaling down my favorite bread recipes taught me a lot about the way bread works and made me a more confident baker. And with each new, tiny golden brown loaf of bread—the perfect amount of bread for me and my husband to share—I found myself thinking "Hmmm . . . other people might love making small loaves of bread, too."

A year after I shared my first small-batch bread recipe—the Loaf Pan Focaccia (page 47)—it suddenly went viral. And kept going viral over and over again. At one point, I was racking up more than one thousand new social media followers a day. My site saw more traffic than it did at the height of the pandemic sourdough craze.

The message was clear: The world needed more small-batch bread recipes.

I quickly got to work on small-batch recipes for ciabatta (page 50), a baguette (page 54), and challah (page 132), which people totally ate up literally and figuratively. Soon, I had a long enough list of bread recipes I wanted to scale down to fill a . . . well, to fill a cookbook.

My goal with this cookbook is to give you the opportunity to try your hand at breadmaking, no matter your skill level. I've broken each recipe into clear, concise steps, with plenty of visual cues to follow along the way. And before you even get to the recipes, I've included a brief overview of common breadmaking terms and techniques so you can feel confident following the recipes and understanding why they work. Whether you continue making small-batch breads or work your way up to full-size recipes, I hope you come away feeling much more confident as a breadmaker.

The best part of these small-batch recipes isn't just that they changed my life. I regularly hear from readers who found breadmaking less intimidating and more accessible with fewer ingredients at risk of waste. And I hear from people who have small kitchens, small families, small freezers, tight budgets, and minimal kitchen equipment, who love that they can also enjoy fresh homemade bread.

And now that you have this book in your hands, I hope these recipes change your life, too.

A BREADMAKING PEP TALK

People have been successfully making bread without fancy equipment and special flours for literally thousands of years. Yes, I am firmly #TeamKitchenScale and encourage you to be precise wherever possible . . . but even when you mess up or don't get it quite right or your loaf turns out looking a little funny, chances are you've still made something edible and tasty. Trust the recipes, banish all negative self-talk, and keep going. What I'm trying to say is: YOU GOT THIS. Those people you see obsessing over dough temperature and fancy flours are trying to achieve very specific, very precise results. You? You just want to make a nice loaf of bread. So don't chase perfection—half the fun is honing your skills as you go. The more bread you make, the better you'll get at making it. Have fun with it!

KITCHEN EQUIPMENT

You don't need a lot of fancy equipment to make these small-batch breads, but having the right tools can make things a lot easier. These are the things I reach for, time and time again, to make the process easier, cleaner, and faster.

Kitchen Scale

A digital kitchen scale is the single most important tool you can add to your kitchen that will immediately make you a better, more consistent baker. Most kitchen scales can switch between metric (grams, kilograms) and US standard (ounces, pounds) measurements. Some kitchen scales struggle to accurately measure small amounts of ingredients (3 grams or less), something that is important when making mini breads. If you're already #TeamKitchenScale but are having trouble with smaller measurements, consider adding a pocket-size jeweler's scale to your kitchen (or use volume measures for small amounts of ingredients). *For more on using a kitchen scale, see Measuring by Weight vs. Measuring by Volume, page 23.*

Mixing Bowl

A 3- or 4-quart bowl can handle any of the recipes in this book. Generally, you want a slightly larger bowl than you think to give yourself more room to mix without flour flying everywhere! I prefer metal or glass bowls, but plastic will also work.

Dough Whisk

A dough whisk (also called a Danish dough whisk) is a stiff, open-wire coil at the end of a long handle. It's a super-efficient way to mix dough by hand, as the wire cuts through and breaks up clumps of flour, quickly combining the dry and liquid ingredients without overmixing. It's also great for mixing quick breads, muffins, and pancake batters!

Bowl Scraper

A bowl scraper is a flat, slightly flexible plastic or silicone scraper with a gently curved edge. It functions as an extension of your hand when mixing or handling dough. The curved edge fits into the side of your bowl, allowing you to scrape it clean as you fold the dough over itself or scrape the dough out of the bowl and onto the counter. These are great tools, especially for anyone who hates the feeling of sticky dough fingers!

Bench Scraper (aka Bench Knife)

A bench scraper is a wide, flat, rectangular metal blade with a grip handle on one side. It's not as sharp as a knife, but it will easily cut through dough. It's incredibly helpful for dividing dough, scraping your work area clean, and lifting shaped dough from your counter to a pan.

Spatula

A small, skinny spatula is great for scraping sticky liquid ingredients like honey out of measuring cups or scoops. Every gram is precious—you don't want to leave any ingredient behind!

Bowl Covers

I usually use clear elastic hair processing caps or shower caps (like the kind you get at a hotel) to cover my bowl while the dough rises. I usually get two to three uses out of each one. For doughs with a shorter rise time (30 minutes or less), a clean kitchen towel draped over the bowl will work, but for anything longer than that, you'll want a cover with a more airtight seal so the dough doesn't dry out. Other reusable bowl cover options include silicone bowl covers and beeswax sheets, or beeswax- or plastic-lined cloth elastic bowl covers.

Rasp-Style Zester

If you want to add finely grated cheese, citrus zest, chile peppers, or nutmeg to your dough, you'll want a long rasp-style zester in your kitchen. The cutting edges are super sharp and create very fine shavings that are easy to incorporate. (They're also handy for sneakily filing down any dark or burned spots that appear on the bottom of your loaves if they end up in the oven a little too long!)

Parchment Paper

Parchment paper helps breads release cleanly from their pans. I love precut sheets for lining pans—quarter- or half-size sheets work great for lining sheet pans or a Dutch oven. To "soften" a sheet of parchment paper so it fits into a round or curved space like a Dutch oven, crumple up the paper, flatten it out, and repeat one more time. Yes, you can use a silicone baking mat on sheet pans, but parchment paper is more versatile, especially when it comes to smaller pans.

Baking Pans

Using the correct baking pan—size and material—is the best way to make sure your breads turn out correctly! Here are the pans I use to make the breads in this book:

- **Sheet Pans:** You can use half-sheet (18 by 13 inches) or quarter-sheet (9 by 13 inches) pans for most of the recipes in this book. For some, an eighth-sheet (about 10 by 7 inches) pan will work, too.

- **Small Square Pullman Pan:** For small sandwich bread–shaped loaves, I use a square, straight-sided metal Pullman pan with a .55-pound capacity (about 4 inches square).

- **Square Baking Dish:** I use a 5 or 6-inch square ceramic or stoneware baking dish for some of the buns and twists like the dinner rolls (page 101).
- **Dutch Oven:** For breads where a crunchy crust matters, the enclosed space of a cast-iron Dutch oven is the best way to get there, as it traps steam on the outer surface of the dough. I use both a 3-quart round and a 7-quart oval Dutch oven for different recipes in this book. If you don't have a Dutch oven, inverting an ovenproof metal bowl over the loaf on a sheet pan will work in a pinch.
- **Baking Steel:** I use a baking steel (also sometimes called a bread steel or a pizza steel) for recipes in this book that require cooking for short periods of time at high temperatures like pizza (page 167), naan (page 141), and pita bread (page 150). Baking bread on a baking steel also helps produce a crispier bottom. I prefer a baking steel over a baking stone because steels get hotter, retain heat better, and are easier to clean. That said, if you have a baking stone, it will work just fine for those recipes. And if you have neither, an inverted sheet pan can work, too.

I don't recommend using glass pans to bake bread. Glass heats slowly, which can make your bread rise unevenly and produces a softer crust, but if you insist, reduce the oven temperature by 25°F and add 5 to 10 minutes to the bake time. Good luck.

Spider Skimmer

A spider skimmer is a wide, round, shallow scoop made of thin wires woven together (like a spider web). In this book it's used for safely lowering, flipping, and removing dough in and out of hot water (for bagels, page 84; or pretzels, pages 88 and 114) or oil (for beignets, page 195). The thin wires and shallow curve of the scoop gently support the dough while allowing water or oil to drip off.

Instant-Read Thermometer

An instant-read probe thermometer is one of the best ways to tell when your bread is done and ready to be removed from the oven. You can also use a thermometer to check the temperature of your water or liquid ingredients to make sure they're just right.

***Fun Fact:** Most bread is done when it reaches an internal temperature of 195° to 205°F.*

Oven Thermometer

Did you know that most ovens aren't calibrated correctly? Some run as much as 30°F hotter or cooler than the built-in temperature gauge indicates. Even worse, some will signal that they're preheated long before they reach the correct temperature. The best way to ensure your oven is at the right temperature is to hang an oven thermometer in the center of your oven.

Misting Spray Bottle

A small misting spray bottle filled with water allows you to quickly spritz the surface of your bread before it goes into the oven for a nice crunchy crust. You can also use the spray bottle to add a tiny amount of moisture to a dough that's feeling a bit dry during the mixing or kneading process, similar to how you would dust in flour during kneading. With these small breads, adding even ½ teaspoon more water to the dough can make a big difference—a misting spray bottle is a great way to add just a touch of moisture without overhydrating the dough.

Flour Duster

I always keep a small shaker filled with all-purpose flour on hand when I'm baking bread, especially when I'm making mini breads. With such small ingredient quantities, dusting in too much flour can dramatically change the texture and hydration of your dough. A flour duster makes it easy to evenly dust down a small amount of flour, so you don't dry out your dough.

Pizza Wheel

A round rolling blade is the best way to cut a pizza (page 167), but also comes in handy for trimming pastry dough edges and for cutting crackers. For fancier zigzag edges, use a fluted pastry wheel, but otherwise a regular old pizza wheel is just fine.

Skillet

A few recipes in this book call for cooking bread in a skillet on the stovetop, such as English Muffins (page 94), Skillet Flatbreads (page 145), and Single Scallion Pancake (page 157). I typically use a 10¼-inch cast-iron skillet because it heats evenly and retains heat well, but you can use whatever skillet you have on hand.

> *If you're using a nonstick skillet, be sure to add the oil BEFORE you preheat the pan. Heating the empty pan can damage the nonstick coating. And never use metal tools on a nonstick surface.*

WHISK
SPIDER SKIMMER
FLOUR DUSTER
PIZZA WHEEL
BENCH SCRAPER
BOWL SCRAPER
KITCHEN SCALE
SQUARE PULLMAN PAN
3-QUART DUTCH OVEN

SQUARE
BAKING
DISH
PARCHMENT
PAPER
PASTRY
BRUSH
LAME
DOUGH
WHISK

BUTTER

INGREDIENTS

Half the magic of breadmaking is that with just a few core ingredients, you can make a whole world of different types of bread. Here are the ingredients I used to develop the recipes in this book and that I try to have on hand at all times—you never know when the urge to bake will strike!

All-Purpose Flour

Most of the recipes in this book use all-purpose flour. True to its name, all-purpose flour is incredibly versatile thanks to its moderate protein content. (When two proteins found in dry flour combine with water, they link up to form the all-important gluten network that gives bread its structure.) All-purpose flour can be used to make everything from pie dough to cookies to cakes to breads. I use King Arthur Baking Company's all-purpose flour, which has a slightly higher protein content (11.9%) than most brands of all-purpose flour (9% to 11%). If you're using a different brand of all-purpose flour with a lower protein content for any of these bread recipes, you may find you get better results with a higher-protein flour from that brand, like bread flour (pie dough and biscuit recipes don't need this adjustment).

Bread Flour

Bread flour has more gluten-forming protein than all-purpose flour, around 12% to 14%, which is why some bread flours are labeled "high gluten" flour. Bread flour is ideal for making things like bagels, pizza, and pretzels where you want a strong crumb, elasticity for shaping, and a chewy texture. I used King Arthur Baking Company's bread flour for the recipes in this book. Bread flour is more absorbent than all-purpose flour, so if you're swapping it into a recipe that calls for all-purpose flour, you may need to add a bit more water to the dough. I only use bread flour when I think it improves the final product enough to justify buying it, so if a recipe calls for it, I definitely recommend using it.

If you're using all-purpose flour in a recipe that calls for bread flour, hold back some of the water and add it in only if the dough seems very dry.

Whole Wheat Flour

Nutty-flavored whole wheat flour has a high protein content (11% to 15%), but contains the bran and germ of the wheat berries, which are sharp and cut through the gluten network you're trying to build. This means that whole wheat breads are often made with a combination of whole wheat and all-purpose flour and tend to feature longer rise times to allow the bran to hydrate and soften. You can use either white whole wheat flour or regular whole wheat flour in any of my recipes that call for whole wheat flour; they are exactly the same, they're simply harvested from different types of wheat, giving them different colors and flavors.

Yeast

I use instant yeast in all of my bread recipes. Instant yeast (sometimes called "rapid rise" or "quick rise" yeast) is one of two types of dry yeast. I prefer instant yeast because you can add it directly to your dry ingredients without having to bloom it in warm water to activate it first, the way you do with active dry yeast. Store your yeast in the freezer to add a year (or more) to its shelf life. You can use it right out of the freezer without having to thaw it. If you're not sure if your yeast is still good, add a bit to a small bowl of warm water mixed with a pinch of sugar—if it foams after a few minutes, it's good!

Diamond Crystal Kosher Salt

Salt doesn't just add flavor to your dough, it also helps control the yeast activity. I use the chef-standard Diamond Crystal kosher salt, which has larger, irregular crystals that dissolve faster compared to other brands and styles of salt. Diamond Crystal kosher salt is also half as salty as other brands of salt *by volume,* so it's always best to measure salt by weight! If you're measuring salt by weight, you can use any type or brand of salt you want. But if you're measuring using teaspoons *and using a different type or brand of salt,* including a different type of kosher salt like Morton kosher salt, **cut the amount of salt in the recipe in half.**

WHAT IF YOU ONLY HAVE ACTIVE DRY YEAST?

The difference between instant yeast and active dry yeast is microscopic: Active dry yeast granules have a little coating around them, which needs to be dissolved (aka bloomed) before the yeast can start working.

If you're using active dry yeast, you have two options:

1. Use the same amount as called for in the recipe and add it with the dry ingredients as instructed. Just know that your dough may take a bit longer (20 to 30 minutes) to rise because the little shell around the active dry yeast granules needs to dissolve before it can start working.

2. Increase the amount of active dry yeast by 25 percent (in recipes this small, that typically means adding 1 gram to the amount the recipe calls for). Instead of adding the yeast to the dry ingredients, stir the yeast into the water the recipe calls for and let it sit for 5 to 10 minutes before using. The rise time should remain the same.

Flaky Salt and Finishing Salts

When it comes to finishing salts, flaky salts like Maldon Sea Salt Flakes, or other flavored salts with large, irregularly shaped crystal flakes are a great way to add a salty crunch to your baked goods. These salts are usually added last and sprinkled on top right before or even after baking; they are not mixed into the dough.

Olive Oil

For baking, I use high-quality, mild-flavored olive oils or extra-virgin olive oils. Some of the brands I like for baking are California Olive Ranch, Kirkland, Brightland, and Filippo Berio. For breads where you want a particular flavor to shine, feel free to use herb- or garlic-infused olive oil instead. And yes, you can use a neutral oil like avocado, canola, or vegetable oil if you don't have olive oil, but you may find your bread ends up a bit bland.

Eggs

I use large eggs in all of my baking. Egg sizes are fairly standard here in the United States, so if you live in a different country or are using a different size egg, this can affect the outcome of your bread—refer to the Volume-to-Weight Conversions chart on page 27 and weigh your eggs if need be. To quickly bring eggs to room temperature, submerge them in hot tap water for 5 to 10 minutes.

Sugar

Granulated white sugar helps add sweetness to your bread. Sugar is more than just a sweetener, however. It also feeds the yeast, contributing to how fast or slow your bread dough might rise, and it also helps dough brown when it cooks.

Brown Sugar

Brown sugar is white sugar mixed with molasses. Dark brown sugar has more molasses than light brown sugar, though they can be used interchangeably in most recipes. The molasses in brown sugar adds flavor, color, and contributes moisture to bread dough.

Honey

In some recipes, I use honey instead of sugar for sweetness. Sometimes this is because the bread is traditionally sweetened with honey, other times it's just preference. Honey is a fairly dense liquid ingredient and weighs a lot by volume. Most of these recipes only use a very small amount; add it slowly—a drop or two at a time—so you don't accidentally add too much!

Milk

I use whole milk in all my recipes. The fat content in whole milk is important for developing a soft, tender, fluffy texture. Substituting a low-fat or fat-free milk will result in bread that is drier and less tender. Your dough will also be wetter, stickier, and harder to handle. I haven't tested my recipes with nondairy milk alternatives, so experiment cautiously if you do!

Butter

The recipes in this book use unsalted American-style butter. Your grocery store's generic, store-brand butter is just fine. American butter contains around 80% butterfat, while European-style butter (e.g., Kerrygold) ranges from 82% to 85% butterfat. Butter contributes water as well as fat to doughs, so I do recommend using the right type of butter; otherwise, you may find the hydration and texture of your dough is off.

Baking Soda

Baking soda (aka sodium bicarbonate) is a chemical leavening agent often used to help cakes and cookies rise. In the world of bread doughs, it's used to give pretzels their signature brown crust and to help leaven some biscuit doughs and flatbreads. To work as a leavener, baking soda must be activated by an acidic ingredient, such as buttermilk or yogurt. Baking soda only has a shelf life of about 6 months, so make sure yours is fresh!

Baking Powder

Baking powder is another chemical leavening agent. It's a combination of baking soda, a dry acid (such as cream of tartar), and a starch to keep the first two ingredients from interacting until you want them to. Baking powder is double-acting, which means it reacts first to moisture and then again to heat, providing a slower and more gentle rise than baking soda.

BREADMAKING TERMINOLOGY

Mixing

Mixing refers to the process of combining the dry and wet ingredients to create a dough. During mixing, the goal is to hydrate the flour and get the ingredients mixed into a cohesive, if lumpy (or "shaggy") dough. A high-hydration dough has a high proportion of water in it and will mix easily using a dough whisk or fork and likely won't require kneading by hand. A lower-hydration dough has a lower proportion of water in it and will quickly absorb all the liquid and may need to be folded over itself several times with a bowl scraper or your hands until all the flour is incorporated and hydrated.

A high-hydration dough has enough water in it that it mixes together easily.

Autolyse

Autolyse might sound like a fancy, complicated French technique, but all it really means is mixing the flour and water together and letting them hang out for a bit before adding the other ingredients. This brief resting period gives the starches in the flour time to align and begin forming a gluten network before any other ingredients are introduced that might inhibit gluten formation. This autolyse step helps to make otherwise sticky doughs more extensible, elastic, and easier to handle.

A low-hydration dough may need to be folded over itself to be sufficiently mixed together.

Kneading

Kneading is one method of working a dough to develop its gluten network. When kneading dough, the dough is repeatedly folded over itself to build strength and structure. During the kneading stage, the dough transforms from a shaggy, lumpy mass into a smooth (or smooth*er*) ball of dough. If the dough looks like it's tearing or not smoothing out, cover it, let it rest for 2 to 3 minutes, then resume kneading. Find examples of different kneading techniques on page 28.

Folding

Folding is another method of developing the gluten network in a bread dough. Instead of kneading, the dough is stretched and folded over itself in the bowl in different directions, with periods of rest in between. It allows the dough to relax and passively build strength as the yeast gets to work.

First Rise/Bulk Fermentation

Bulk fermentation refers to the dough's first rise. Most doughs rise in two stages–the first is when it rises as one large "bulk" of dough. Some doughs require a series of folds performed at regular intervals during the bulk fermentation stage to build strength into the dough.

Proofing/Rising

Proofing refers specifically to the second rising stage of a dough, which usually takes place after the dough has been shaped but before it is baked. That said, it's also used colloquially as a catch-all term to refer to the process of dough-rising in general, as dough can be underproofed or overproofed during both bulk fermentation and proofing.

Resting

Resting allows the dough's gluten network to relax and get used to a new shape, and also gives the starches time to fully hydrate and align, building strength into the dough. These resting periods make the dough easier to shape and handle. Some doughs may not rise during a rest period, but that doesn't mean the rest isn't necessary; there's still plenty happening inside the dough!

The Fingerprint Test

The fingerprint test is a way to check if your dough is properly proofed. Gently press a lightly floured finger into the surface of your dough.

- If the indentation fills back in quickly and completely, the dough needs more time. Check again every 10 to 15 minutes until it's ready.
- If your finger leaves a visible indent that fills back in so slowly you can hardly see it, the dough is proofed and ready for the next step.
- If the dough deflates completely when you press it, it's overproofed. Womp-womp.

TEMPERATURE AND BREADMAKING

Temperature is one of the main factors in determining how quickly or slowly your dough will rise. This includes the temperature of the ingredients in your dough, as well as the temperature of the room where your dough is rising. In baking, "room temperature" is generally somewhere around 72°F.

- Warmer temperatures increase yeast activity.
- Cooler temperatures slow down yeast activity.

If your dough is rising slowly *and* your kitchen is cold, find somewhere warmer to put your dough during the resting periods. I have a seed starting heat mat that I got for less than $15 that I put my bowl of dough on in the winter.

If your kitchen is very warm, your dough might be a lot more active and ready to bake sooner than the times given in the recipe. If your dough is rising *too* quickly in your warm kitchen, put it in the fridge for all or part of the rise time to slow it down.

Just because the dough isn't "ready" right at the time given in a recipe doesn't mean it's not working—there might be other factors affecting how quickly or slowly it gets there! You may need to make adjustments to the timing.

Scoring

Scoring means slashing the top of your loaf of bread before baking. Scoring is both functional and decorative. It creates a vent for steam to escape as the bread bakes; without it, the steam will force its way through any weak points in the dough, including the seam at the bottom. You can use a *lame* (French for "blade," pronounced "lahm"), which is essentially a razor blade with a handle, or a sharp knife for scoring. The angle at which you score your loaf, as well as the depth of the cut, will determine how the bread expands in the oven. Play around with different angles to see how it affects your final loaf!

MEASURING BY WEIGHT Vs. MEASURING BY VOLUME (and How to Do Both!)

The recipes in this book include both weight (grams) and volume (cups, tablespoons, teaspoons) measurements. I *strongly* encourage you to use the weight measurements (#TeamKitchenScale). But if you're going to use volume measurements, I've included detailed instructions for how to measure them as accurately as possible.

I know, I know, here in the United States, we're a bit late to the kitchen scale party, but it's catching on—with good reason! Measuring ingredients by weight is the most accurate way to measure baking ingredients. *Making that switch is the single most effective way to immediately become a better, more consistent, and more confident baker.*

If you've been measuring using cups and have wondered why sometimes a recipe turns out perfectly, and other times the same recipe turns out flat or dense or the dough is just way too sticky or dry, measuring by weight will help fix that problem.

Did you know that there's no universally accepted standard for what 1 cup of flour weighs? Unlike denser ingredients like water, honey, or even granulated sugar, which can fill a measuring cup with few to no air pockets, flour is light and can be loosely or tightly packed into a measuring cup depending on how it's scooped. One baker's "1 cup" of flour may weigh 120 grams. Another baker's "1 cup" of flour may weigh 200 grams. That's a big difference!

Another reason to measure by weight? No need to mess with finicky fractions or limit yourself to predetermined common measurements. A lot of recipes in this book call for 1 gram of yeast. That's ⅓ teaspoon. Do *you* have a ⅓ teaspoon in your kitchen? Probably not!

Every recipe in this book was developed with weight measurements first. When it comes to bread recipes this small, being off by even a few grams can make a big difference in the final bake, so *I really do recommend using a kitchen scale for the best results.*

TARE g
120
TARE
HOLD
UNIT
Escali

How to Use a Digital Kitchen Scale

Most digital kitchen scales have two main buttons. One is a TARE button (this is also sometimes the ON/OFF button) and the other is a UNIT CONVERSION button, which allows you to switch between US standard (ounces/pounds) and metric (grams/kilograms) measurements.

1. Turn the kitchen scale on and place the bowl you're using on top of it.
2. Hit the TARE button. The TARE button puts a zero back on the kitchen scale, removing the weight of whatever is already on the scale.
3. Add your first ingredient to the bowl and weigh it.
4. Hit the TARE button again. The scale is now back to zero and ready for you to add your next ingredient.
5. Repeat until all your ingredients are in the bowl.

When adding liquid ingredients to dry ingredients, the best practice is to measure them into a separate cup or bowl and then pour them into the dry ingredients. If you accidentally add too much of a liquid ingredient to the dry ingredients already in the bowl, it's pretty hard to remove without taking some of the dry ingredients as well!

One of the biggest reasons people fall in love with measuring ingredients by weight is because you can weigh ingredients right into the bowl, without having to wash more measuring spoons or cups. Fewer dishes to wash is always a win in my book. And this is *my book.*

How to Measure as *Accurately as Possible* by Volume

If you insist on measuring your ingredients by volume, it is super important that you measure the ingredients properly. Use dry measuring cups for dry ingredients and a liquid measuring cup for liquid ingredients. Measuring spoons work for small amounts of dry or liquid ingredients.

How to Measure Flour by Volume

Stir and fluff the flour in your flour container well, so there's plenty of air in it. Use a spoon to gently scoop the flour into the measuring cup, then sweep any excess off the top using the back of a knife. The cup should feel pretty light and the flour should *not* be tightly packed into it.

How to Measure Sugar by Volume

Tightly pack granulated white or brown sugar into the measuring spoons or cups, so there are no air pockets trapped inside.

DICTIONARY CORNER

- **Heaping:** A heaping cup, tablespoon, or teaspoon is scooped so that the ingredient domes just slightly over the rim of the scoop.
- **Scant:** A scant cup, tablespoon, or teaspoon is filled to just below being completely full. A bit less than the full scoop.

How to Measure Liquids by Volume

Use a liquid measuring cup (the kind with a spout). Place it on a level surface and fill it until the liquid reaches the correct marker when looking at it at eye level.

How to Measure with Measuring Spoons

Scoop dry ingredients flat against the rim or edge of the container, or use the back of a knife to sweep the excess off the top. Liquid ingredients should not overflow the rim of the measuring spoon unless otherwise specified.

Scoop aerated flour into the dry measuring cup.

Sweep the excess flour off the top with the back of a knife. It's okay if there are some air pockets at the top.

VOLUME~TO~WEIGHT CONVERSIONS

There is no set standard for what 1 cup of flour weighs. It's a huge problem, I know! Different recipe developers and brands use different conversions. The table below lists the volume-to-weight conversions I used for the most common ingredients in this book.

INGREDIENT	VOLUME	WEIGHT
FLOUR (bread/all-purpose)	1 cup	120g
WATER or MILK	1 cup	240g
	½ cup	120g
	⅓ cup	80g
	¼ cup	60g
	1 tablespoon	15g
	1 teaspoon	5g
DIAMOND CRYSTAL KOSHER SALT	1 teaspoon	3g
	1 tablespoon	9g
INSTANT YEAST	1 teaspoon	3g

INGREDIENT	VOLUME	WEIGHT
SUGAR (brown/white)	1 teaspoon	4g
	1 tablespoon	12g
OIL (olive, vegetable, etc.)	1 teaspoon	4g
	1 tablespoon	12g
BUTTER	1 tablespoon	14g
WHOLE EGG (US large egg, out of the shell)	1 egg	50g
EGG YOLK (US large egg)	1 yolk	17g to 18g
HONEY	1 teaspoon	7g
	1 tablespoon	21g

Adapted from King Arthur Baking Company.

BREADMAKING TECHNIQUES

The recipes in this book are too small for the average stand mixer, and hand mixers just don't cut it when it comes to making dough. Instead, you'll be using a variety of techniques to develop strength and structure (aka the all-important gluten network) in these mini bread doughs. Some require kneading, others use methods like folding, and others just use time. Some even use a combination of a few of these techniques. ***Bookmark this section, you'll be coming back here often!***

Kneading by Hand

Hand kneading is what most of us think of when we picture making bread. When kneading dough by hand, you fold, rock, and/or roll the dough against the counter as it smooths out, strengthens, and develops a strong gluten network. It's best for lower-hydration doughs that aren't too sticky.

With any kneading method, lightly dust in additional flour *only as needed* if the dough is *really* sticking to your hands or the counter. Use a bench scraper if you need to scrape up stuck dough or scrape your hands clean as you work. The dough should stick less as it develops more strength, so you don't want to add *too much* flour to the dough if it's not called for. If the dough feels like it's fighting you, tears, or isn't smoothing out as you knead, cover it with a damp paper towel and let it rest for 2 to 3 minutes, then resume kneading.

> *Kneading by hand can be tough on the arms. Set a timer to keep yourself honest so you know you've kneaded for as long as the recipe says.*

METHOD 1: ROCK AND FOLD

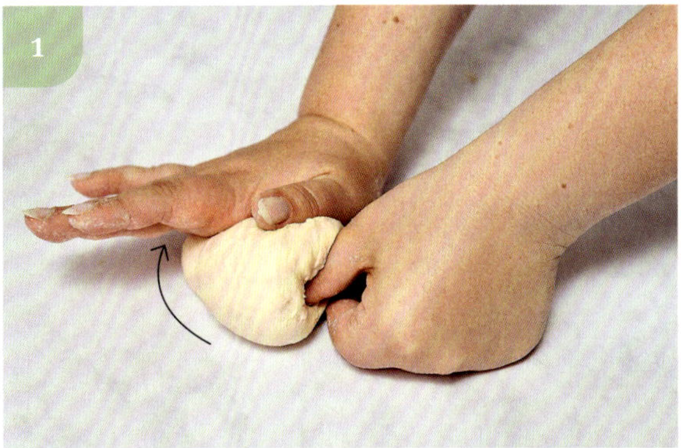

Use the thumb from your nondominant hand to hold the dough in place while you fold the top edge of dough down.

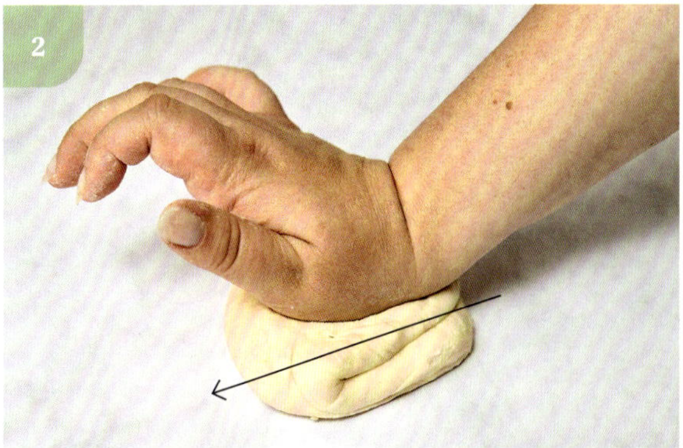

Press down with the heel of your hand to seal the folded dough shut, then rock the dough forward.

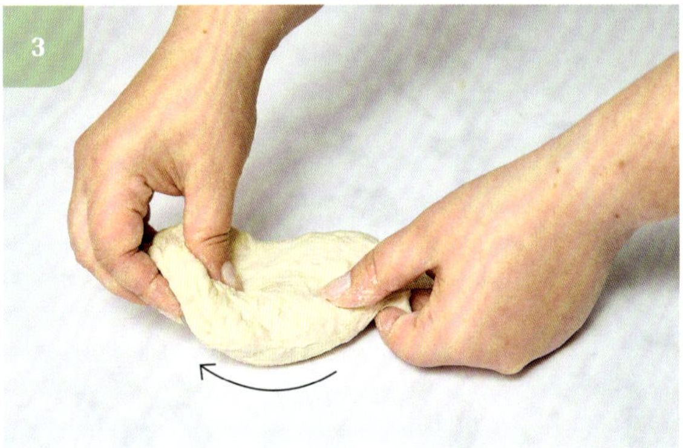

Rotate the dough 90 degrees. Repeat.

METHOD 2: CRISS-CROSS

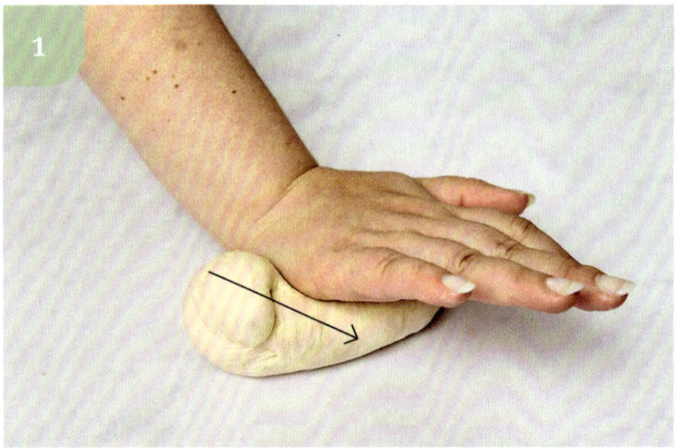

Roll the dough with the heel of your right hand, moving diagonally away from your body from right to left.

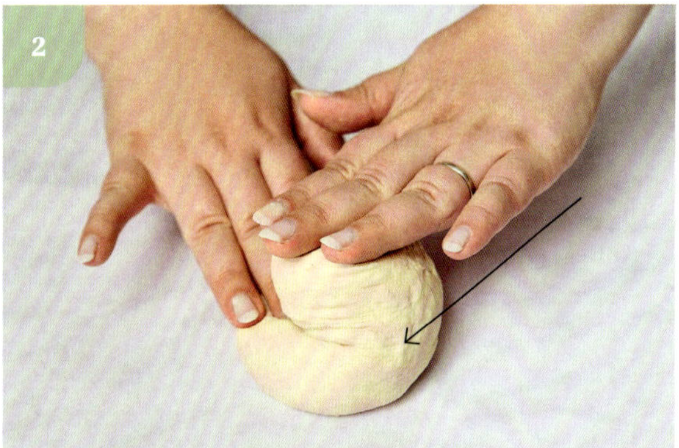

When your right arm is extended, roll the dough with your left hand, moving diagonally away from your body from left to right.

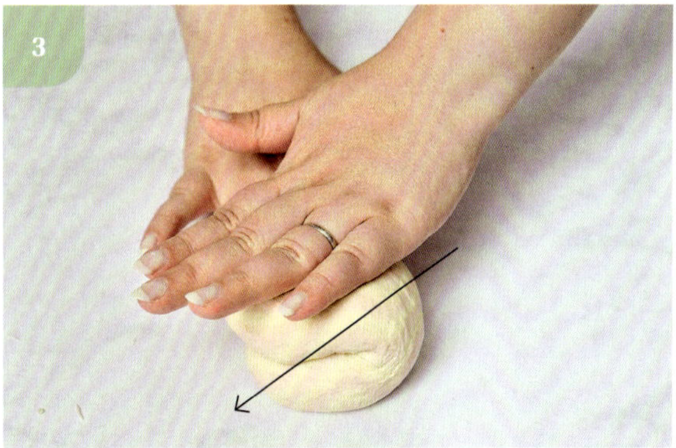

As you roll forward, press on the top of the log of dough, folding it over itself as it rolls. Repeat.

Slap and Fold

The "slap and fold" is one way to add structure and strength to bread doughs in place of kneading. It's particularly useful for sticky, high-hydration doughs.

Usually, this is done on a countertop, where the dough is slapped down to stretch out the gluten strands, then folded over itself to build structure. Because these recipes are so small, I do the slap and fold right in the bowl. Use a damp hand to prevent the dough from sticking to you.

Just because it's called "slap" and fold doesn't mean it has to be aggressive. If the dough is slippery, it might not stick to the bowl with a satisfying "slap." As long as you're repeatedly folding the dough over itself in different directions, you're doing it right!

Scoop up the dough with the fingers of your dominant hand.

Slap the dough against the bottom or side of the bowl.

Fold the dough away from you and over itself.

Rotate the bowl a quarter-turn. Repeat steps 1 through 4 four to six times. This completes one set of folds.

Stretch and Fold

The stretch and fold is a gentler version of the slap and fold. Instead of lifting the dough out of the bowl for each fold, you stretch the dough out before folding it over itself. Again, use a damp hand to prevent the dough from sticking to you.

To keep track of what set of folds you're on, place a small bowl with a number of candies or snacks in it that corresponds to the number of folds. Eat one each time you do a set of folds. When you eat the final candy, you know you've done the last set of folds!

Stretch the top edge of the dough away from you.

Fold it down over itself.

Rotate the bowl 90 degrees (a quarter-turn). Stretch the new top edge of dough away from you.

Fold the dough down over itself. Repeat steps 1 through 4 four to six times. This completes one set of folds.

Biscuit Method

The biscuit method is used for making flaky doughs (often yeast-free) like pie dough (page 181), scones (page 179), and biscuits (pages 172 and 176). When following a recipe made using the biscuit method, it's important to keep your butter and your liquid ingredients cold!

The flaky layers in these recipes are created when the water in the cold butter turns to steam in the oven. The steam pushes the layers of dough apart, creating that flaky texture.

Biscuit Notes and Tips

- The bigger the pieces of butter in the dough, the flakier the final product. The more you work the dough, the smaller the pieces will become. Pinching the butter and kneading the dough together is fun, but don't overdo it!
- Work quickly when pinching the butter into the dry ingredients; even the heat from your hands can make the butter melt.
- If you don't want to or can't use your hands to pinch the butter, you can use a pastry cutter or pastry blender (a set of U-shaped blades or wires) to cut the butter into the dough instead.
- If the dough starts to feel warm or greasy or the butter feels like it's melting, stick the dough in the fridge or freezer to cool down. This will allow the butter to firm up again.

Shaping a Tight Ball (Boule)

Shaping a tight, round *boule* (that's French for "ball") is a technique you'll use over and over again throughout this book. There are several techniques for doing this, so if you have a preferred method, use it. Unless otherwise specified, this method works best on a clean, unfloured surface.

Shaping a larger ball of dough works the same way, only instead of one hand you'll use both to gently lift and rotate the dough against the counter, almost in a bouncing motion, using your pinkie fingers to tuck the edges of the dough under to create that surface tension on top.

Gently deflate the piece of dough.

Tuck or fold all the edges in.

If needed, pinch the edges together at the bottom to seal them shut. This may not be necessary for wetter, looser doughs.

Place the seam against the counter, cup your hand around the dough with your pinky finger flush against the counter, and move in quick circular motions to tighten up the seam.

If you need to combine a few pieces of dough to make your boule the correct size, stack the smaller pieces on top of the biggest piece before deflating it so that the smaller pieces end up tucked inside.

Shaping a Batard

A batard is an oval or oblong-shaped loaf of bread. A batard can have tapered, pointed ends or blunt, round ones. It's up to you!

Stretch the dough into a loose rectangle shape.

Fold the top two corners in to make a point at the top.

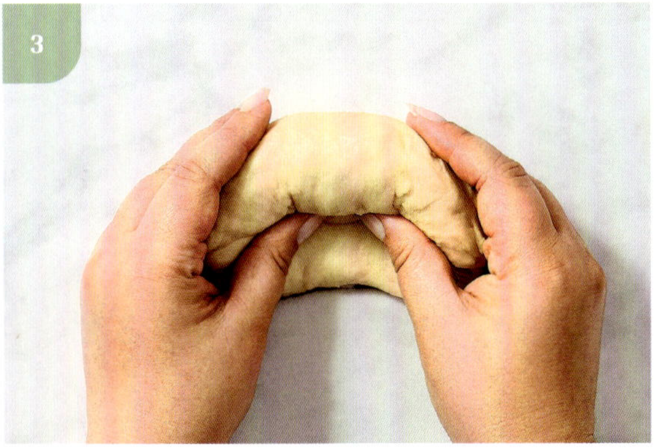

Roll the point toward you, folding the two sides in as you roll until you have a log of dough with all the edges tucked under.

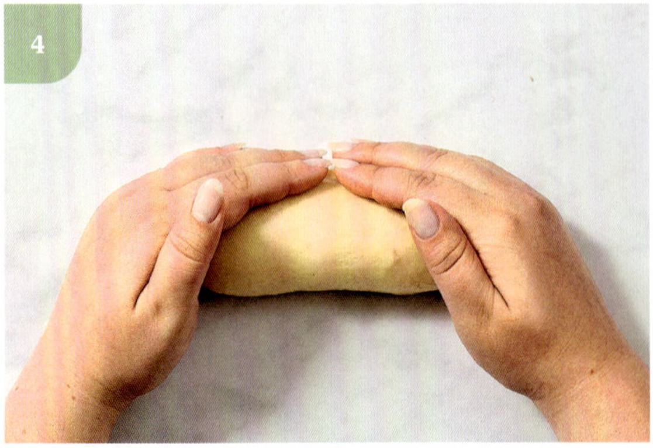

Roll the batard until the seam is underneath. Cup your hands around the back of the loaf and pull it toward you to create surface tension and tighten the seam underneath.

SOURDOUGH CORNER

While I haven't personally tested all of the recipes in this book with sourdough starter, I didn't want to leave you without the option to give it a try on your own.

Using Sourdough Starter or Sourdough Discard Plus Instant Yeast

To incorporate 100% hydration active sourdough starter or sourdough discard into any of these small-batch bread recipes, start by replacing 10 grams of the water and 10 grams of the flour in the recipe with 20 grams of sourdough starter/discard OR simply add 20 grams of sourdough starter/discard to the dough along with the liquid ingredients. The recipes will still need the instant yeast for the timing to work, and may need a bit more flour or water added to reach the right consistency, but the starter will add a nice sourdough flavor!

Using *Only* Sourdough Starter

To leaven any of the recipes in this book using *only* active, fed sourdough starter and no instant yeast, you'll have to do a bit of experimenting. A general rule of thumb is that you can add up to 20% of the flour by weight in starter. For most of the recipes in this book, that's 24 grams. Hold back about 12 grams of water or liquid from the recipe to start, and add it in gradually if the dough needs it.

You'll have to experiment with different kneading and rising times, or different cadences of folding during the first rise to build the strength the dough needs. Sourdough is a much slower process than dry yeast–leavened breads, so be patient and good luck!

ADDING FLAVORS

You can customize many of the recipes in this book with different flavorings and mix-ins. Here are a few guidelines to get you started:

- Add no more than 36 grams of heavy mix-ins, such as seeds, nuts, fruits, vegetables, cheeses.
- Add no more than 1 tablespoon of lighter mix-ins, such as herbs, zests, spices, powders, extracts.
- If adding a seasoning blend (e.g., everything bagel seasoning), check the ingredient list; if it includes salt, reduce the amount of salt in the recipe.
- Wet ingredients, such as olives, peppers, tomatoes, and onions will add some moisture to your dough, so you may need to add a bit more flour or hold back a little bit of water.
- Dry ingredients (herbs, spices) may create a drier dough, so you may need to add a bit more water during mixing.
- Adding ingredients may slow down yeast activity, so follow the visual cues for doneness in the recipe if the dough seems to be moving slower than expected.

SCALING UP

I know, I know, why would you scale *up* a small-batch bread recipe? The whole point is that they're small! But this is one of the most common questions I get when people fall in love with these mini breads, so I want to make sure you know how to do it if you want.

Most recipes can be easily doubled or tripled just by doubling or tripling the ingredients. However, many of these small-batch recipes use relatively large quantities of yeast proportional to the flour, and if you increase the yeast at the same rate as the rest of the ingredients, your dough may rise much, much faster than expected.

While every other ingredient can be doubled, tripled, or even quadrupled just fine, when it comes to the yeast, I recommend increasing the amount by no more than **1 gram for every additional cup of flour.** *However,* if you're scaling up one of the no-knead breads or other doughs with minimal kneading and a long rise, you shouldn't need more than 2 grams of yeast max—even if you quadruple the recipe.

When in Doubt . . .

- If your dough seems too dry, add water a ¼ teaspoon at a time.
- If your dough seems too wet, add flour a pinch at a time.
- If your dough is rising slowly, put it somewhere warm or let it rise longer until it matches the description in the recipe.
- If your dough is rising too quickly or you need to slow it down, put it somewhere cold.
- If you live somewhere very humid or that gets a lot of rain, hold back 5 to 10 grams of water and add it only if needed.
- If your dough is too sticky to handle, try lightly flouring your hands. If that doesn't work, try using damp or lightly oiled hands.
- If your dough is shrinking back a lot or not stretching as much as it should, cover and let it rest for a few minutes, then try again.

Just to Say It

All bodies are good bodies, it's okay to be fat, and it's wonderful to enjoy your food and to make food you enjoy eating. Though this is a book about small breads, I don't ever talk about food in a restrictive way, and there are so many reasons to make these small-batch breads other than being afraid you'd eat "too much" of a full-size loaf. You worked hard to bake bread, you deserve to enjoy eating it! I hope you enjoy these recipes as a way of finding joy and creativity in your kitchen—and that you don't feel guilty about eating them either!

CHAPTER 1

LITTLE LOAVES

OVERNIGHT NO-KNEAD CRUSTY BREAD

MAKES
1 SMALL LOAF

RISING TIME:
8 TO 12 HOURS

BAKE TIME:
30 MINUTES

120g (1 cup) all-purpose flour + more for dusting

3g (1 teaspoon) Diamond Crystal kosher salt

1g (heaping ¼ teaspoon) instant yeast

100g (⅓ cup + 4 teaspoons) cool water (70°F)

It doesn't get more basic than this. If you're looking for a classic white crusty bread with a moderately open crumb, this is the recipe for you. Four ingredients, no kneading, and you can totally ignore it while the yeast gets to work overnight. This is the easiest, most hands-off method for developing your dough's gluten network. It's also the longest, as you're relying on time to develop strength and structure in your dough. It's almost like magic—you mix up a messy ball of dough at night, and the next day it'll have a bubbly, flat top, ready to be shaped and baked. The final loaf bakes up about the size of a large grapefruit and is great for snacking, dipping, and dunking—it can even work as a bread bowl for soup.

1. **Mix and rest.** In a medium bowl, whisk together the dry ingredients. Add the water and use a dough whisk or a fork to mix until a sticky dough forms (photo 1). Gather the dough in a messy ball in the bowl. Cover the bowl and let the dough rest at room temperature for 8 to 12 hours (overnight) OR in the refrigerator for at least 24 hours or up to 5 days. Perfectly proofed no-knead dough will have a bubbly top that is flat or slightly domed and stretches across the entire bowl (photo 2).

2. **Preheat.** When you're ready to bake, preheat the oven to 450°F with a covered Dutch oven inside for at least 30 minutes. Crumple a sheet of parchment paper, flatten it out, and set it aside nearby.

3. **Shape**. While the Dutch oven preheats, generously flour a clean surface. Release the dough from the sides of the bowl and turn it onto the floured surface. Dust the top lightly with flour, just enough so your hands don't stick. Shape the dough into a ball following the instructions with photos 3 and 4. (If you'd like to shape the dough into a batard, see page 36.)

4. **Second rest.** Use a bench scraper to help lift the ball of dough onto the parchment paper. Dust the surface of the dough lightly with flour, cover it with a clean kitchen towel or invert the bowl over it, and let it rest until the Dutch oven finishes preheating, 20 to 30 minutes.

5. **Score**. Immediately before baking, score the top of the loaf with one deep slash and any decorative slashes you desire. If the dough seems too sticky to score, refrigerate it, uncovered, on a sheet pan for 15 to 20 minutes before scoring—the gluten will tighten up in the cold.

recipe continues

6. **Bake**. Carefully remove the Dutch oven from the oven. Gather the corners of the parchment paper together, pick up the loaf, and place it inside the Dutch oven. Put the lid back on and bake, covered, for 20 minutes (don't peek!). Remove the lid and bake, uncovered, until browned on top, about 10 minutes. Transfer the loaf to a wire rack and let it cool completely before slicing.

OVERNIGHT NO-KNEAD WHOLE WHEAT BREAD

70g (½ cup + 2 teaspoons) all-purpose flour + more for dusting

50g (⅓ cup + 2 teaspoons) whole wheat flour

3g (1 teaspoon) Diamond Crystal kosher salt

1g (heaping ¼ teaspoon) instant yeast

102g (⅓ cup + 1½ tablespoons) cool water (70°F)

Whole wheat flour on its own is notoriously bad at developing a gluten network strong enough to support a whole loaf of bread without being quite dry, so to make a whole wheat version of this little loaf you'll use a blend of whole wheat and all-purpose flours. Blending whole wheat with all-purpose flour and giving the dough plenty of time to rise makes for a crusty loaf with a slightly open crumb and a mild yet nutty whole wheat flavor. For this loaf, I pushed the amount of whole wheat flour as high as I could, landing around 42% whole wheat flour to 58% all-purpose flour. I also upped the amount of water to account for the fact that whole wheat flour absorbs more water than white flour does—no one is baking dry bread on my watch!

Follow the directions for Overnight No-Knead Crusty Bread.

After mixing, the dough will be very sticky and messy.

After its long rest, the dough will have a bubbly, flat top that stretches across the bowl. If your dough has overproofed, it will appear sunken in and the edges of the dough will be sloped down in the bowl. Slightly overproofed no-knead dough can still be shaped and baked—it'll just produce a flatter loaf.

Stretch the dough into a loose square. Fold all the edges in and across each other in the middle of the dough, pressing them together to seal.

Flip the dough over so the pinched-together seam is underneath. Lift and rotate the dough, tucking the edges under as you go to create more surface tension on top.

LOAF PAN FOCACCIA

MAKES ONE
8 BY 4-INCH LOAF

RISING TIME:
2½ HOURS

BAKE TIME:
20 TO 25 MINUTES

120g (1 cup)
all-purpose flour

5g (1 teaspoon
+ a heaping ½ teaspoon)
Diamond Crystal
kosher salt

5g (1¼ teaspoons)
sugar

3g (1 teaspoon)
instant yeast

90g (⅓ cup + 2 teaspoons)
warm water (90°F)

10g (2½ teaspoons)
+ 6g (1½ teaspoons)
olive oil + more
for drizzling

Cooking spray

Pinch of flaky sea salt
and/or fresh herbs,
for topping

Affectionately known to readers of *The Practical Kitchen* as "the mini bread that could," this adorable golden-brown mini focaccia was the first small-batch bread I ever made, and it went *mega-viral.* It's also the bread recipe that has proven to so many people that they *can* successfully make bread.

If you're looking for a great place to start your epic breadmaking journey, this salty, airy, crisp-bottomed mini focaccia is a great place to begin. Eat it plain, slice it into breadsticks, serve it up as a sandwich, turn it into focaccia artwork (you can get very creative with your toppings here), or even use it to make a mini thick-crust pan pizza.

1. **Mix.** In a medium bowl, whisk together the dry ingredients. Make a well in the center and add the warm water and 10 grams of the olive oil. Use a dough whisk or a fork to stir the liquid in the center, slowly incorporating flour from the sides of the bowl until a sticky dough forms. Use a bowl scraper or your hand to fold the dough over itself, rotating the bowl as you go, until the dough is lumpy, cohesive, and no sneaky dry spots of flour remain. Gather the dough in a messy ball in the bottom of the bowl. Cover the bowl and let the dough rest for 15 minutes.

2. **First set of folds.** Use a damp hand to perform a series of slap and folds (see page 30) in the bowl until it feels like the dough has tightened up slightly. Cover the bowl and let the dough rest for 15 minutes.

3. **Second set of folds.** Repeat the slap and fold process. The dough will still be sticky, but should feel smoother and stronger.

4. **Rise.** Spray an 8 by 4-inch metal loaf pan with cooking spray, then drizzle in the remaining 6 grams olive oil. Transfer the dough to the pan so the seam side is down. Use lightly oiled fingers to gently prod the dough into a rough rectangle shape in the pan. Cover the pan and allow it to rise somewhere warm until the dough *almost* covers the bottom of the pan (photo 1), about 1 hour.

5. **Preheat.** During the final 30 minutes of rise time, preheat the oven to 400°F.

recipe continues

6. Dimple and top. Drizzle the dough with a little more olive oil, then use oiled fingers to dimple the dough following the instructions in photos 2 and 3. Cover the pan and let the dough rise until the dimples fill in slightly and the dough looks airy, another 15 to 20 minutes. Sprinkle with a pinch of flaky salt and/or any toppings you like.

7. Bake. Bake until golden brown on top, 20 to 25 minutes. Remove from the oven and immediately turn the focaccia out onto a wire rack so the bottom doesn't get soggy. Let it cool at least 10 minutes before slicing.

FOCACCIA TOPPING INSPIRATION

- Fresh rosemary or other herbs + flaky sea salt
- Thinly sliced apples + shredded cheddar cheese
- Cherry tomatoes + thinly sliced red onions + goat cheese crumbles
- Mozzarella + pepperoni + cherry tomatoes
- Everything bagel seasoning + goat cheese crumbles
- Green olives + thinly sliced roasted red pepper + feta cheese crumbles
- Thinly sliced Honeynut squash + shredded cheddar cheese + fresh rosemary

If topping your mini focaccia with lots of cheese or moist ingredients, slide the loaf pan onto a preheated baking steel or inverted sheet pan to ensure a crispy bottom.

1

After rising, the dough will fill out more of the pan, but still might not fill it out entirely.

2

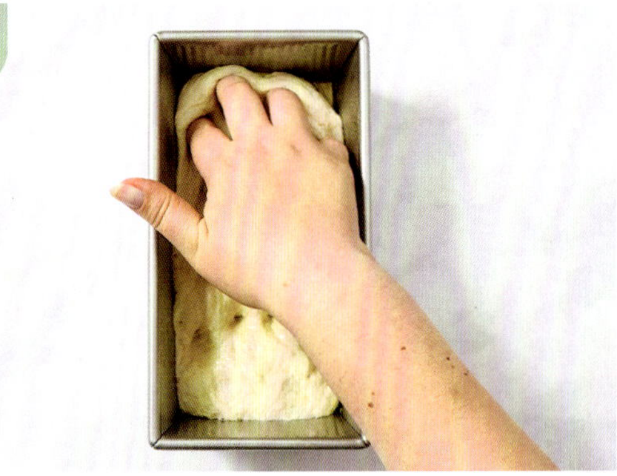

Use your oiled fingers to dimple the dough. Press down to the bottom of the dough, spreading your fingers out to push the dough into the corners of the pan.

3

Dimple generously! And don't pop the air bubbles!

FREEFORM CIABATTA

MAKES
1 SMALL LOAF

RISING TIME:
2½ HOURS

BAKE TIME:
20 TO 22 MINUTES

Ciabatta, Italian for "slipper," is a relatively new Italian bread (it was invented by a miller named Arnaldo Cavallari in the 1980s) known for its chewy, flour-dusted crust and airy interior crumb. It's perfect for sandwiches or dipping in your favorite seasoned oils. And the best part? Shaping is minimal here—plop the dough out and bake it whole, or cut it into rolls, or even breadsticks.

120g (1 cup)
all-purpose flour
+ more for dusting

3g (1 teaspoon)
Diamond Crystal
kosher salt

3g (1 teaspoon)
instant yeast

105g (⅓ cup
+ 5 teaspoons)
warm water (90°F)

5g (1¼ teaspoons)
olive oil

1. **Mix.** In a medium bowl, whisk together the dry ingredients. Make a well in the center and pour in the warm water and olive oil. Use a dough whisk or a fork to mix until a sticky dough forms. Gather the dough into a ball in the bottom of the bowl, cover the bowl, and rest for 20 minutes.

2. **First set of folds.** Use a damp hand to perform a set of stretch and folds (see page 31), followed by a set of slap and folds (see page 30). Cover the bowl and let the dough rest for 20 minutes.

3. **Second set of folds.** Perform another set of stretch and folds, followed by another set of slap and folds. Cover the bowl and let the dough rest for another 20 minutes.

4. **Third set of folds.** Perform a final set of stretch and folds and slap and folds in the bowl. Finish by tucking all the edges under the dough, creating a nice smooth surface on top. The dough should feel much airier and won't stretch as much as it did on the earlier sets of folds. Cover the bowl and let the dough rest for 30 minutes this time—it will spread out and rise in the bowl, but may not double in size.

5. **Preheat.** While the dough rests, preheat the oven to 450°F. Line a sheet pan with parchment paper.

6. **Shape.** Dust the top of the dough in the bowl with flour, then gently tip it out onto the prepared sheet pan (the sticky side will be facing up). Dust the sticky top side of the dough lightly with flour. Cover the dough with a clean kitchen towel and let it rest for about 10 minutes. (You can also shape your ciabatta into rolls or breadsticks by following the photos.)

7. **Bake.** Dust any excess flour off the top, then bake the ciabatta until it's puffed up and browned on top, 18 to 19 minutes for a soft ciabatta, or 20 to 22 minutes for a crustier ciabatta. Let it cool completely before slicing. Regardless of how long you bake it, ciabatta will seem very hard when it first comes out of the oven, but will soften as it cools.

THREE WAYS TO SHAPE CIABATTA

To shape one whole ciabatta loaf, turn the dough out and prod it gently into a loose oval shape, just enough to even out the thickness across the loaf.

To create **pull-apart ciabatta rolls,** use a bench scraper or a sharp knife to divide the dough into quarters but DON'T separate the pieces before baking. If you want individual ciabatta rolls, nudge them apart on the sheet pan and reduce the bake time by 3 to 5 minutes.

To create **ciabatta breadsticks,** loosely prod the dough into a roughly 5 by 8-inch rectangle, then cut it lengthwise into 1-inch-wide strips and place them 1 to 2 inches apart on the sheet pan. Reduce the bake time by 3 to 5 minutes.

FOOT-LONG(-ISH)
BAGUETTE

FREEFORM
CIABATTA

FOOT~LONG(~ISH) BAGUETTE

MAKES ONE
10- TO 12-INCH
BAGUETTE

RISING TIME:
2½ HOURS

BAKE TIME:
20 TO 23 MINUTES

120g (1 cup)
all-purpose flour
+ more for dusting

3g (1 teaspoon)
Diamond Crystal
kosher salt

3g (1 teaspoon)
instant yeast

96g (⅓ cup
+ 1 tablespoon)
warm water (90°F)

What better way to take an imaginary trip to Paris than with a baguette for one? I was so broke when I visited Paris while studying abroad in college that my friend Laura and I bought a single jar of jam that we carried around with us—baguettes were affordable, so we'd stop and pick up a baguette each morning for breakfast, tearing chunks of it to dip in the jam. While I admit this baguette is nowhere near as refined as one you'd get in France, if you're a beginner baker or just want to practice your baguette-shaping skills, this recipe will get you pretty dang close! The shaping technique takes time to master, so go easy on yourself!

While the size and shape of a 7- to 9-quart oval Dutch oven will create the best, crustiest mini baguette, you can also bake it in a large round Dutch oven (at least 11 inches in diameter), on a sheet pan with an inverted roasting pan on top, or simply on a sheet pan. To create a steamier environment (for a crunchier crust) without a Dutch oven, toss a couple of ice cubes on the sheet pan and into the oven when you add the baguette.

1. **Mix and rest.** In a medium bowl, whisk together the dry ingredients. Make a well in the center and pour in the warm water. Use a dough whisk or a fork to mix until a sticky dough forms. Gather the dough into a messy ball in the bottom of the bowl. Cover and let the dough rest for 30 minutes.

2. **First set of folds.** Perform a set of stretch and folds (see page 31). Flip the dough so the seam side is down. Cover and let rest for 30 minutes.

3. **Second set of folds.** Repeat the stretch and folds, again finishing by flipping the dough so the seam side is down. Cover the bowl and let the dough rest for 1 hour this time. The dough will double or triple in size and become quite bubbly and airy.

4. **Preheat.** Toward the end of the rise time, preheat the oven to 450°F with a covered 7-quart oval Dutch oven inside.

5. **Shape.** Dust the top of the dough with flour, then turn it out onto a lightly floured surface. Dust the top of the dough lightly with flour, just enough to keep it from sticking to your hands. Shape the baguette following the instructions in photos 1 through 4. Use a bench scraper to help fold and maneuver the dough if you need to. The dough will naturally elongate as you work through the shaping process.

recipe continues

Loosely stretch the dough into a rectangle on a lightly floured work surface.

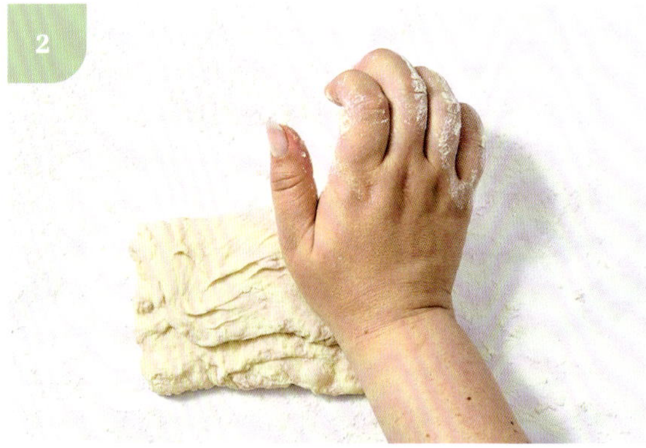

Fold the top third down and use the heel of your hand to gently but firmly seal the edge shut.

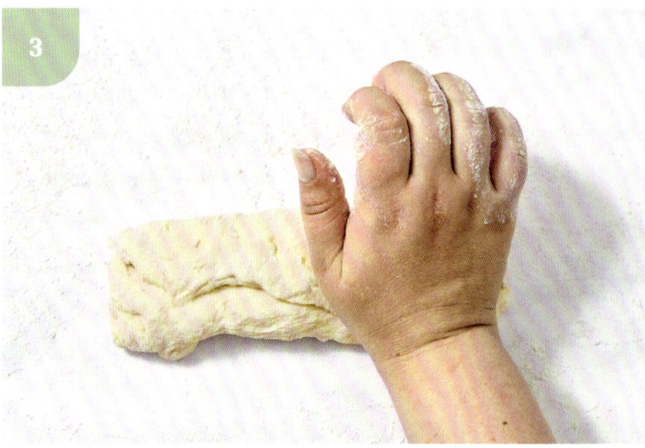

Rotate the dough 180 degrees so the folded edge (not the seam) is now at the bottom. Fold the top third down again and seal the edge with the heel of your hand.

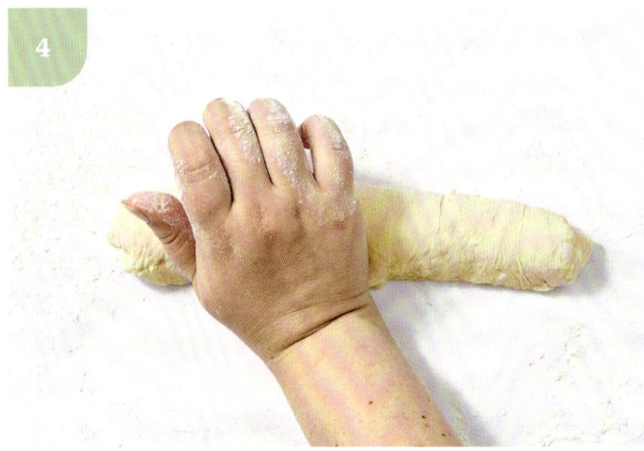

Fold the new top edge down, this time folding the dough in half. Use the heel of your hand to seal the edges together against the counter.

6. Taper. Roll the dough so the pinched seam is underneath, then follow the instructions in photos 5 and 6 to even out the baguette's thickness and taper the ends.

7. Second rest. Dust a clean kitchen towel with flour and gently lift the baguette onto it. Pinch the towel along either side of the baguette so it stands up along the length of the dough (photo 7). Cover the baguette with plastic wrap or place it (on a sheet pan) inside a large plastic bag to prevent it from drying out. Let it rest for 30 minutes. During this time, fill a small spray bottle with water, get out your lame or a sharp knife, and clear a space with a trivet to put the hot Dutch oven.

8. Score. Remove the plastic and use the kitchen towel to gently roll the baguette onto a sheet of parchment paper so it lies on a diagonal. Score along the length of the baguette—you can do one long slash or three offset vertical slashes (photo 8). Spray the baguette generously with water.

9. Bake. Carefully place the hot Dutch oven on the trivet. Lift the parchment paper from the two open corners, creating a sling for the baguette, transfer the baguette and the parchment to the Dutch oven, and cover immediately. Bake, covered, for 10 minutes (don't peek!). Uncover and bake 10 minutes. Then, if your baguette needs a bit more color, bake for an additional 2 to 3 minutes directly on the oven rack. Transfer the baked baguette to a wire rack and let cool completely before slicing.

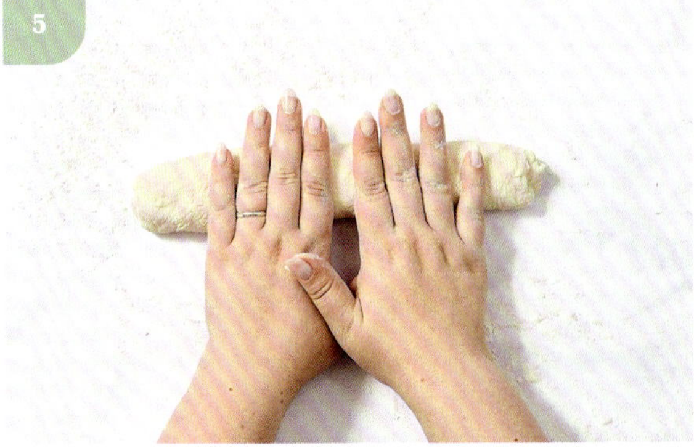

Making sure the pinched seam is underneath, roll the dough once or twice with gentle pressure from the center outward to even out the baguette.

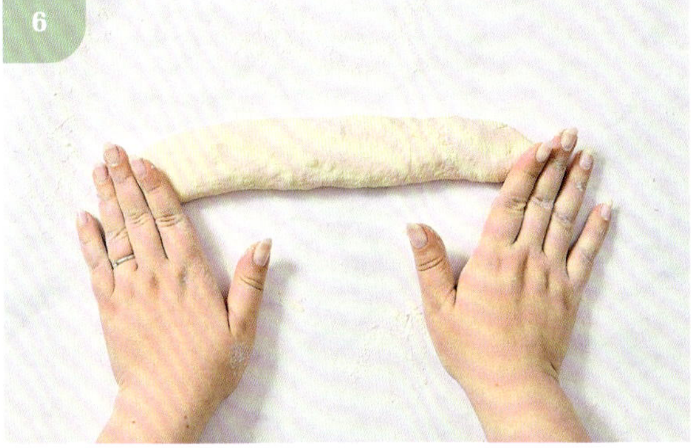

Taper the ends by rolling them with your hands angled so your pinkies are flush against the counter.

Use a floured kitchen towel to support the baguette during its final rise: Pinch the towel so it stands up along either side of the baguette. (Optional: Use binder clips at the tapered ends to hold the towel in place.) Cover the baguette so it doesn't dry out.

Score one long lengthwise slash or three 3- to 4-inch lines down the length of the baguette.

FOUR~INCH SANDWICH BREAD

MAKES
1 SMALL LOAF

RISING TIME:
2 HOURS

BAKE TIME:
20 TO 22 MINUTES

To make a small-batch sandwich bread that's tall enough for a satisfying sandwich, we're going to ignore the fact that every other recipe in this book calls for 120 grams (1 cup) of flour. Put your fingers in your ears and sing la-la-la-la, okay? In this case, scooping 180 grams of flour (1½ cups, by my math) is more than worth it for producing a towering loaf of soft white sandwich bread with a golden crust. I can usually get 4 to 6 good slices out of it, 8 if I eat the bread butts (and I always eat the bread butts).

180g (1½ cups)
all-purpose flour
+ more for dusting

9g (2 teaspoons)
sugar

3g (1 teaspoon)
instant yeast

3g (1 teaspoon)
Diamond Crystal
kosher salt

110g (⅓ cup
+ 2 tablespoons)
warm water (90°F)

8g (2 teaspoons)
olive oil

Cooking spray

1. **Mix.** In a medium bowl, whisk together the dry ingredients. Make a well in the center and add the warm water and olive oil. Use a dough whisk or a fork to mix until a sticky dough forms, then use a bowl scraper or your hand to fold the dough over itself until it comes together and all the dry bits are incorporated.

2. **Knead**. Turn the dough out onto a lightly floured surface and use a very light touch to briefly knead the dough just to help fully hydrate the dry ingredients, 30 to 60 seconds. It will feel stickier than most bread doughs you knead, but should pull fairly cleanly away from the counter. A little sticking is fine, just scrape it up and add it back to the dough if it happens. If things are very sticky, dust in a tiny amount of flour.

3. **First rise**. Shape the dough into a loose ball, tucking the edges under. Lightly grease the bowl with cooking spray, then place the dough inside, cover, and let rise for 30 minutes.

4. **Fold.** Perform a set of slap and folds (see page 30). (This is a lower-hydration dough, so it won't stretch much.) Cover the bowl and let rise for another 30 minutes.

5. **Shape**. Turn the dough onto a barely floured counter. Shape following the instructions in photos 1 through 3. Lightly grease a 4-inch square Pullman loaf pan with cooking spray. Place the roll of dough inside with the seam facing down.

6. **Second rise.** Cover the top of the pan loosely with plastic wrap and let it rise somewhere warm until the top of the dough just barely reaches the top rim of the pan, about 1 hour (if your kitchen is cold, it may need up to 30 minutes more).

7. **Preheat**. During the final 30 minutes of rising, preheat the oven to 375°F.

8. **Bake**. Bake until the loaf is golden brown on top, 20 to 22 minutes. Immediately turn the bread out of the pan and onto a wire rack. Let cool completely before slicing.

Press or roll the dough into a roughly 8 by 5-inch rectangle.

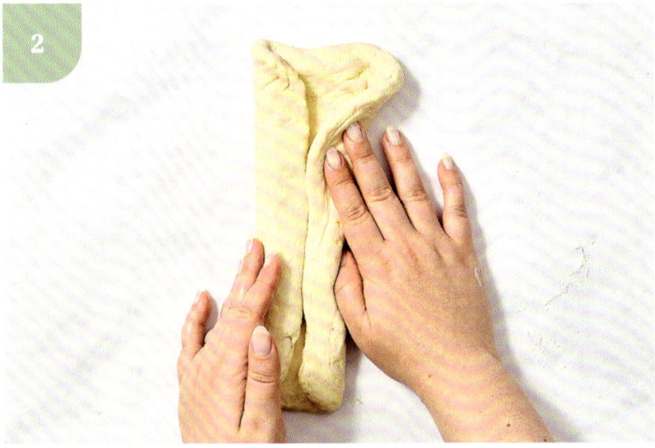

Fold the two long sides in about 1 inch so you have a long narrow strip of dough about 3 inches wide.

Starting with one of the short ends, roll the dough up into a tight coil.

NO-KNEAD
PEASANT BREAD

FOUR-INCH
SANDWICH
BREAD

NO-KNEAD PEASANT BREAD

MAKES
1 SMALL LOAF

RISING TIME:
1 HOUR 20 MINUTES

BAKE TIME:
25 TO 28 MINUTES

120g (1 cup)
all-purpose flour

3g (1 teaspoon)
instant yeast

2g (heaping ½ teaspoon)
Diamond Crystal
kosher salt

2g (½ teaspoon)
sugar

110g (⅓ cup
+ 2 tablespoons)
warm water (90°F)

14g (1 tablespoon)
unsalted butter,
at room temperature

This little loaf of buttery white bread is a riff on one of my favorite weeknight breads: Alexandra Stafford's peasant bread, which is *so* popular it became the focus of her 2017 cookbook *Bread, Toast, Crumbs* and has over one thousand five-star reviews on her website, the kind of numbers food bloggers dream of! Thanks to the hands-off no-knead mixing method and fast rise time, it's a lovely everyday bread that's wonderful sliced and buttered for snacking but also so good for dunking in soups, mopping up spaghetti sauce, and more.

While Alexandra's recipe calls for baking the loaf in a buttered ovenproof glass bowl, I've provided a bowl-free baking method in case you don't have a bowl in the right size (see recipe notes). Her recipe also calls for using forks to handle the dough, but I found I had more success with spoons—you do you!

1. Mix. In a medium bowl, whisk together the dry ingredients. Make a well in the middle and pour in the warm water. Use a dough whisk or a fork to mix until a sticky, messy dough forms. Gather the dough into a loose ball in the bottom of the bowl.

2. First rise. Cover the bowl and let the dough rise until it doubles in size, 1 to 1½ hours. The top will be bubbly and flat.

3. Grease. Toward the end of the rise time, grease a 1- to 1½-quart ovenproof glass bowl generously with the softened butter.

4. Shape. Use spoons or a small spatula to gently release the dough around the edges and gather them into the middle of the dough (photo 1). Use two spoons to lift the dough out of the mixing bowl and plop it into the buttered glass bowl (photo 2). Don't worry about it looking pretty!

5. Second rise. Cover the bowl and let the dough rise until it looks a little airier and relaxed, 20 to 30 minutes. (It won't double in size, but will fill out the bottom of the bowl a little more.)

6. Preheat. While the dough rises, preheat the oven to 425°F.

7. Bake. Place the bowl on a sheet pan and slide it into the oven. Bake for 10 minutes at 425°F, then, *without opening the oven*, reduce the oven temperature to 375°F and bake until golden brown on top, another 15 to 18 minutes. Carefully turn the baked peasant bread out of the bowl and onto a wire rack to cool–it should slide right out thanks to the butter! Let the loaf cool for at least 15 to 20 minutes before slicing.

Recipe Notes

- I use the glass bowl Alexandra recommends to bake this bread: the Pyrex 322 1-quart glass bowl, which is ovenproof and has a great shape for supporting the bread as it rises and bakes.

- You can also bake this peasant bread on a sheet pan—brush the outside generously with 1 tablespoon melted butter before baking. The final loaf won't be as tall or as round, but will still taste great.

- To customize the flavors of your peasant bread, you can add up to 1 tablespoon of seeds, cheese, herbs, or minced peppers, onions, sun-dried tomatoes, etc. to the dry ingredients in step 1.

After the first rise, the dough will have a flat, bubbly top. Use spoons or a small spatula to release the edges and pull them into the middle of the bowl.

Use two spoons to lift the dough and plop it into the buttered glass bowl for baking.

DRESSING UP BRIOCHE

- **Add flavors:** For a sweeter brioche, add ¼ teaspoon vanilla extract with the wet ingredients in step 1. For a brioche loaf that skews toward fall/winter flavors, add ¼ teaspoon ground cinnamon to the dry ingredients in step 1. You can also brush the freshly baked brioche with garlic butter or honey butter while it's still warm from the oven.
- **Add toppings:** After brushing with the egg wash in step 9, sprinkle the brioche with pearl sugar, sesame seeds, everything bagel seasoning, poppy seeds, rolled oats, flaky sea salt, or any other toppings you like.

CLASSIC BRIOCHE LOAF

MAKES
1 SMALL LOAF

RISING TIME:
2 TO 4 HOURS

BAKE TIME:
20 MINUTES

120g (1 cup)
all-purpose flour
+ more for dusting

3g (1 teaspoon)
instant yeast

4g (1 teaspoon
+ heaping ¼ teaspoon)
Diamond Crystal
kosher salt

15g (1 tablespoon)
whole milk,
***warmed* (90°F)**

10g (1½ teaspoons)
honey

1 large egg, *at room temperature*

28g (2 tablespoons)
unsalted butter,
at room temperature

Cooking spray

Egg wash:
1 large egg,
beaten well

Buttery, soft brioche is a classic enriched dough. It's super versatile and can be used to make everything from the pretty oval loaf that you see here, to recipes you'll find later on in this book like Mini Chocolate Babka (page 135) and Honey-Butter Brioche Dinner Rolls (page 101).

Brioche dough is kneaded twice—first without the butter, and then again to incorporate the butter. If you were to mix everything all at once, the butter would coat the flour and prevent it from absorbing the other liquids in the dough and forming that all-important gluten. The first knead gives the dough time to form a strong gluten network without the butter. The second allows the softened butter to coat the gluten network. Though it's a messy journey once the butter is introduced, it's so worth it for the end destination—a smooth, soft, and supple dough that is a dream to work with.

1. **Mix.** In a medium bowl, whisk together the dry ingredients. Make a well in the center and add the warm milk, honey, and egg. Use a dough whisk or a fork to mix until all the liquid is absorbed. Use a bowl scraper or your hand to fold the dough over itself in the bowl until all the dry bits are incorporated.

2. **Knead.** Turn the dough out onto a lightly floured counter and knead until fully hydrated, 2 to 3 minutes. This is a *dense* dough and won't feel very elastic to knead, so really put your weight into it.

3. **Rest.** Tuck the dough into a loose ball and place it back in the bowl. Cover the bowl and let the dough rest for 10 minutes.

4. **Knead in the butter.** Kneading in the butter gets messy and takes time. Set a timer to keep yourself honest, and follow the instructions in photos 1 through 4 to knead the dough until the butter is incorporated and the dough smooths out.

5. **First rise.** Tuck the dough into a ball, lightly grease the bowl with cooking spray, and return the dough to the bowl. Cover and let the dough rest in a warm spot until it passes the Fingerprint Test (page 20), 1 to 2 hours.

recipe continues

6. Shape. Turn the dough out onto a clean work surface. Gently deflate with your fingertips and shape the dough into a batard (see page 36) or a boule (see page 34). Brioche is very sensitive to temperature: If it's warm in your kitchen or you just run hot, dust the dough *lightly* with flour as needed to prevent it from sticking OR pop the dough in the fridge for 10 to 15 minutes prior to shaping to help the butter in the dough firm up.

7. Second rise. Line a sheet pan with parchment paper. Place the shaped brioche loaf on the prepared pan, cover loosely with plastic wrap, and let rise until doubled in size, 1 to 2 hours. The dough should look puffy and a little airy and should spring back when you poke it gently.

8. Preheat. Toward the end of the rise time, preheat the oven to 350°F.

9. Bake. Brush the egg wash lightly all over the dough, making sure to get the sides and along the bottom of the loaf where it meets the pan. Bake until golden brown and shiny on top, 20 to 25 minutes. Transfer the brioche to a wire rack and let cool completely before slicing.

Recipe Note

Because brioche has a lot of butter in it, warmer temperatures (even just the warmth from your hands) can make the dough stickier to handle. You can use the cold temperature of your fridge to firm up the butter (making the dough easier to handle) by popping the dough in for just 10 minutes. Or you can use it to slow down the rise in step 5—place the dough in the fridge for at least 3 hours or up to 48 hours prior to shaping it. Refrigerated brioche dough will likely need a longer rise time in step 7, so plan accordingly. Brioche is best baked from room temperature.

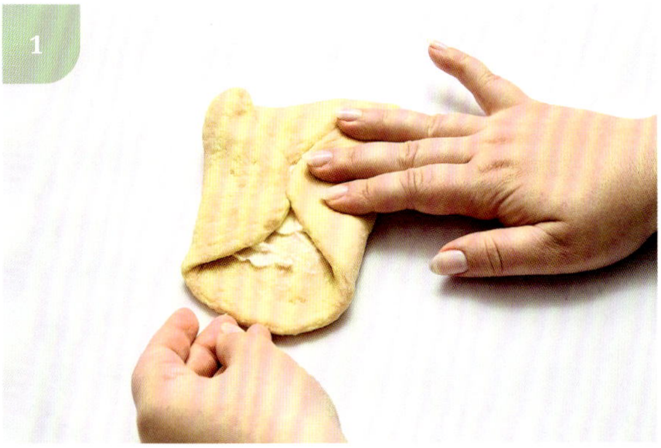

Stretch the dough into a 6- to 7-inch square. Spread the surface with half the softened butter, then fold all the edges in and pinch them together. Spread the top of the dough with the remaining butter and fold the dough around it again.

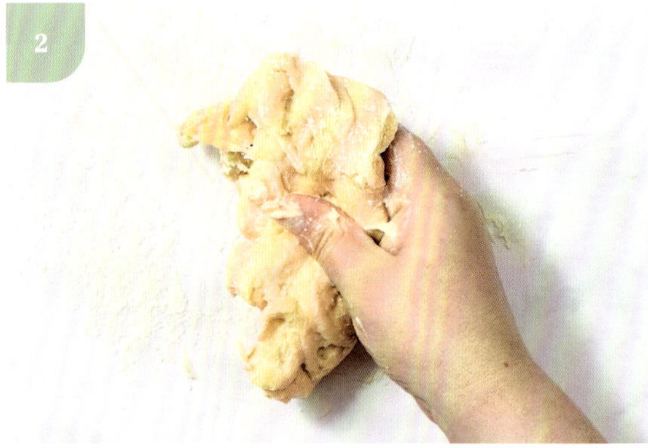

Knead the dough, embracing the mess as the butter slips and slides all over the place and the dough falls apart. You will think it's gone wrong; I promise it hasn't. Dust in flour very lightly as needed to help the butter incorporate.

Smear the dough and butter on the work surface with the heel of your hand, gather it up with a bench scraper, squish it in your fingers, fold it over itself, and keep kneading until the butter absorbs into the dough. This whole process can take 5 to 6 minutes.

Once the butter has fully incorporated into the dough, dust the work surface lightly with flour and knead until smooth and supple, another 2 to 3 minutes.

DELI~STYLE SEEDED RYE BREAD

MAKES
1 SMALL LOAF

RISING TIME:
2½ HOURS

BAKE TIME:
20 TO 25 MINUTES

Given my initials spell R-Y-E, I've always had an affinity for Jewish deli-style rye breads, the kind loaded with caraway seeds. To soften the caraway seeds and infuse the dough with a more mellow caraway flavor, the first step of this recipe is one of the most useful things I learned in pastry school: making a simple caraway seed tea. Because rye flour is incredibly thirsty and terrible at developing a gluten network, for this recipe we're using a blend of 25% rye flour and 75% all-purpose flour, with a dough that clocks in at a whopping 95% hydration! A 10-minute autolyse gives the starches time to hydrate and for the gluten network to start forming before adding any ingredients that will tighten them up (like salt), making for a dough that is soft, strong, and holds its shape well.

CARAWAY SEED TEA

100g (⅓ cup + 4 teaspoons) hot water (160°F), *NOT boiling*

10g (4 teaspoons) caraway seeds

AUTOLYSE

90g (¾ cup) all-purpose flour + more for dusting

30g (¼ cup) rye flour

TO FINISH

15g (1 tablespoon) warm water (90°F)

5g (1 heaping teaspoon) olive oil

4g (heaping ½ teaspoon) honey

3g (1 teaspoon) instant yeast

3g (1 teaspoon) Diamond Crystal kosher salt

1. **Make the caraway seed tea.** In a heatproof liquid measuring cup, mix the caraway seeds and hot water. Let sit for 10 minutes or until the temperature of the mixture reaches below 110°F (do not strain).

2. **Autolyse.** In a medium bowl, combine the all-purpose flour, rye flour, and caraway seed tea (including the caraway seeds). Use a dough whisk or a fork to mix until a messy dough forms. Use a bowl scraper or your hand to fold the dough over itself in the bowl until it's stiff and shaggy. Cover the bowl and let the dough rest for 10 minutes.

3. **To finish the dough.** While the dough rests, in a small bowl, mix the warm water, olive oil, honey, and yeast to give the yeast a head start and make it easier to mix into the dough. Cover and set aside until the autolyse is done. The yeast mixture will get very foamy and bubbly.

4. **Add the salt and yeast.** Sprinkle the salt over the dough in the bowl, then pour the foamy yeast mixture on top (photo 1). Use your hands to pinch, squish, and fold the dough over itself until the yeast mixture and salt are incorporated and the dough no longer feels grainy (photo 2). The dough will be VERY wet. Do your best to shape it into a loose ball in the bowl, then cover and let rest for 30 minutes.

5. **First set of folds.** Use a damp hand to perform a set of slap and folds (see page 30) in the bowl. Cover and let the dough rest for 30 minutes.

6. **Second set of folds.** Repeat the slap and fold process. Cover and let the dough rest for another 30 minutes.

7. **Third set of folds.** Repeat the slap and fold process one more time—the dough will feel much stronger at this point. Cover the dough and let it rest for another 30 minutes. The dough will just about double in size and become quite airy; it might even have some visible bubbles on top.

8. **Shape.** Gently turn the dough out onto a generously floured surface. Dust the top of the dough lightly with flour, just enough to keep your hands from sticking. Shape the dough into a batard (see page 36).

9. **Rise.** Line a sheet pan with parchment paper. Transfer the dough to the prepared sheet pan. Dust the top of the dough lightly with flour, then cover loosely with plastic wrap or a clean kitchen towel. Let rise until just about doubled in size, 30 minutes to 1 hour.

10. **Preheat.** Toward the end of the rise time, preheat the oven to 400°F.

11. **Bake.** Use a lame or a sharp knife to slash the top of the rye loaf 3 to 4 times on a diagonal. Bake until the top begins to brown, 20 to 25 minutes. Transfer the loaf to a wire rack and let cool completely before slicing or tearing into it!

Recipe Note

If you prefer not to have caraway seeds in your rye bread, use a fine-mesh sieve to strain the seeds out when you pour the tea into the flour mixture in step 2. You'll get caraway flavor without the seeds.

Pour the salt onto the dough, followed by the foamy yeast mixture.

Squish and fold the dough over itself until all the yeast and salt are absorbed and the dough no longer feels grainy.

SOFT BROWN BREAD

MAKES
1 SMALL LOAF

RISING TIME:
2 TO 2½ HOURS

BAKE TIME:
20 TO 25 MINUTES

Inspired by everyone's favorite tableside bread course at the one and only factory of cheesecake, this soft brown bread gets its rich color from the tiniest bit of cocoa powder in the dough. It's a little bit sweet, a lot a bit savory, has a slightly nutty flavor from the whole wheat flour, and is absolutely perfect served warm with a pat of honey butter.

80g (⅔ cup)
all-purpose flour
+ more for dusting

40g (⅓ cup)
whole wheat flour

3g (1 teaspoon)
instant yeast

3g (1 teaspoon)
Diamond Crystal
kosher salt

3g (1 scant teaspoon)
natural unsweetened
cocoa powder

60g (¼ cup)
warm water (90°F)

28g (2 tablespoons)
unsalted butter,
melted

21g (1 tablespoon)
honey

Egg wash: 1 large egg,
beaten well

Pinch of rolled oats
(optional), for topping

1. **Mix.** In a medium bowl, whisk together the dry ingredients. Make a well in the center and add the warm water, melted butter, and honey. Use a dough whisk or a fork to mix until all the liquid is absorbed. Switch to a bowl scraper or your hand and fold the dough over itself until all the dry bits are incorporated.

2. **Knead.** Turn the dough out onto a lightly floured counter and knead until smooth and slightly tacky to the touch, about 2 minutes. Apply very little pressure to the dough while kneading and lightly dust more flour onto the counter as needed just to prevent sticking.

3. **First rise.** Place the dough back into the bowl, cover, and let rest somewhere warm until the dough passes the Fingerprint Test (page 20), 1 to 2 hours. The dough will grow but may not truly double.

4. **Shape.** Plop the dough out onto a lightly floured work surface. Gently smush and stretch it into a long rectangle shape. Shape it into a long batard (see page 36) with the seam underneath.

5. **Second rise.** Line a sheet pan with parchment paper. Place the loaf on the prepared pan, cover loosely with plastic wrap, and let rise until just about doubled in size, 1 to 1½ hours.

6. **Preheat.** During the final 30 minutes of rise time, preheat the oven to 350°F.

7. **Egg wash.** Brush the egg wash lightly all over the dough. Sprinkle the top with rolled oats, if using.

8. **Bake.** Bake until dark brown and shiny on top, 20 to 25 minutes. Transfer to a wire rack and let cool slightly before eating. This loaf is best enjoyed warm!

CHAPTER 2

BUNS AND ROLLS

ONE LARGE KAISER ROLL

MAKES
1 KAISER ROLL

RISING TIME:
2 HOURS

BAKE TIME:
13 TO 15 MINUTES

DOUGH

120g (1 cup)
all-purpose flour
+ more for dusting

3g (1 teaspoon)
Diamond Crystal
kosher salt

2g (½ teaspoon)
sugar

2g (heaping
½ teaspoon)
instant yeast

60g (¼ cup)
warm water (90°F)

10g (scant 1 tablespoon)
olive oil

Cooking spray

TOPPING

Milk wash:
1 tablespoon whole milk

Poppy seeds, sesame seeds, dried minced onion, or everything bagel seasoning

Hailing from Austria, kaiser rolls (sometimes called Vienna rolls) are round, slightly flat, dense rolls with a thin crust. They're often used for breakfast sandwiches and deli sandwiches, where they're stuffed with corned beef, pastrami, or roast beef, but are also great for sloppy joes, burgers, pulled pork, and fried chicken sandwiches.

To shape a kaiser roll, some people roll a long rope and twist it into a knotted, flower-like shape, others roll the dough into a ball and use a stamp to create the signature curved petal shape, while others (hello, it's me!) prefer to score the design into the top. This dough will work with any of those shaping methods, but I find scoring is easiest for getting uniform results. Need more than one kaiser roll? You can divide this dough in half to make two smaller kaiser rolls without changing the bake time.

1. **Mix.** In a medium bowl, whisk together the dry ingredients. Make a well in the center and add the warm water and olive oil. Use a dough whisk or a fork to mix until the dough forms large clumps with bits of dry flour still in the bowl. Switch to a bowl scraper or your hand and fold the dough over itself in the bowl until it comes together—it's okay if there are still some dry bits left, they'll incorporate in the next step.

2. **Knead.** Turn the dough out onto a lightly floured surface and knead until smooth and soft, about 2 minutes. Resist adding more flour unless absolutely necessary.

3. **First rise.** Lightly grease the bowl with cooking spray. Shape the dough into a ball, return it to the greased bowl, cover, and let it rest somewhere warm until the dough passes the Fingerprint Test (page 20), 1 to 1½ hours.

4. **Shape.** Line a sheet pan with parchment paper. Shape the dough into a tight ball (see page 34). Place it seam-side down on the prepared sheet pan.

5. **Second rise.** Set the kaiser roll up for its second rise following the instructions in photos 1 and 2.

6. **Preheat.** Toward the end of the rise time, preheat the oven to 425°F.

7. Bake. Immediately before baking, brush the milk over the roll, add any toppings, and use a lame or sharp knife to score the roll top, following the instructions in photos 3 and 4. Bake until lightly browned on top, 13 to 15 minutes. Let the kaiser roll cool completely on a wire rack before slicing.

Spray the top of the roll lightly with cooking spray, then loosely cover with plastic wrap. Place another sheet pan on top of the dough and gently press down until the bottom of the sheet pan barely reaches the top rim of the bottom sheet pan.

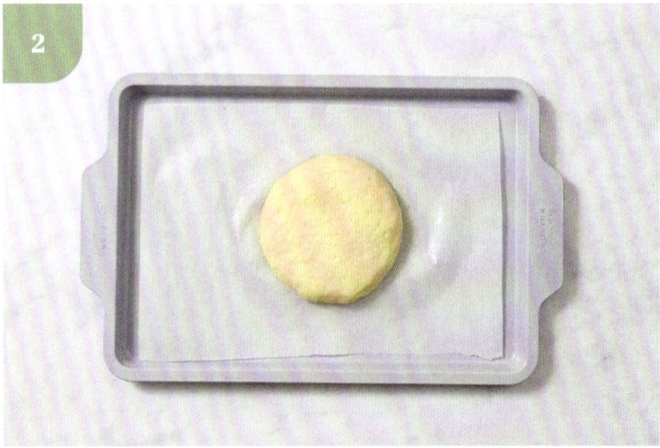

Set the pan aside to rise in a warm spot—with the sheet pan on top—until the dough springs back when you tap it with a fingertip, 1 to 1½ hours. The roll should look visibly puffy, almost but not quite doubled in size.

Immediately before baking, remove the top sheet pan and plastic wrap and brush the kaiser roll with the milk.

Sprinkle roll with any desired toppings. Score 5 slightly curved lines about ¼ inch deep arcing from the center of the roll out.

ONE LARGE
KAISER ROLL

ALMOST
FOOT-LONG
HOAGIE ROLL

ALMOST FOOT~LONG HOAGIE ROLL

MAKES
1 ROLL

RISING TIME:
2 HOURS

BAKE TIME:
14 TO 16 MINUTES

My ideal hoagie roll is soft and squishy with a pale golden brown, shiny crust that spiderwebs into cracks around your fingertips when you pick it up. Rather than using my usual technique for rolling a long narrow loaf of bread, this recipe borrows a gentler technique from self-proclaimed food antagonist Joe Rosenthal: The dough is loosely shaped into a round, folded in half, pinched together, and then gently rolled into shape without deflating it too much.

120g (1 cup)
all-purpose flour
+ more for dusting

4g (1 teaspoon + heaping ¼ teaspoon)
Diamond Crystal kosher salt

3g (1 teaspoon)
instant yeast

2g (½ teaspoon)
sugar

80g (⅓ cup)
warm water (90°F)

5g (1¼ teaspoons)
olive oil + more for greasing

Egg wash: 1 large egg, *beaten well*

1. **Mix.** In a medium bowl, whisk together the dry ingredients. Make a well in the center and add the warm water and olive oil. Use a dough whisk or a fork to mix until the dough forms large clumps with bits of dry flour still in the bowl, then switch to a bowl scraper or your hand and fold the dough over itself in the bowl until it comes together—it's okay if there are still some dry bits left, they'll incorporate in the next step.

2. **Knead.** Turn the dough out onto a lightly floured surface. Dust the top of the dough lightly with flour. Knead with a very light touch just until the dough starts to smooth out, 1 to 2 minutes. The dough will feel dry at first, but as soon as it starts to feel a little sticky, shape it into a loose ball.

3. **First rise.** Lightly grease the bowl with olive oil. Return the dough to the greased bowl, cover, and let rest in a warm spot until it doubles in size and passes the Fingerprint Test (page 20), 1 to 1½ hours.

4. **Shape.** Carefully turn the dough out onto a very lightly floured surface (less is more when it comes to flour here). Do not flour the top of the dough. Shape the hoagie roll following the instructions in photos 1 through 3.

5. **Second rise.** Line a sheet pan with parchment paper. Place the shaped hoagie roll on the prepared pan and cover loosely with plastic wrap. Let rise until just about doubled in size and the dough looks airy and springs back when you poke it, 45 minutes to 1 hour.

6. **Preheat.** Toward the end of the rise time, preheat the oven to 400°F.

7. **Bake.** Immediately before baking, brush the roll all over with the egg wash. Score according to the directions in photo 4. Bake until pale golden brown, 14 to 16 minutes. Transfer the roll to a wire rack and let cool completely before slicing. (The hoagie roll will be hard at first but will soften as it cools.)

Recipe Note

For a crisper crust, skip the egg wash and let the shaped hoagie roll do its second rise *and* bake in a perforated baguette pan on a sheet pan. This allows airflow around the roll in the oven, producing a harder crust.

Use your fingertips to gently prod and press the dough into a round shape 8 to 9 inches across with the sticky, unfloured side of the dough facing up.

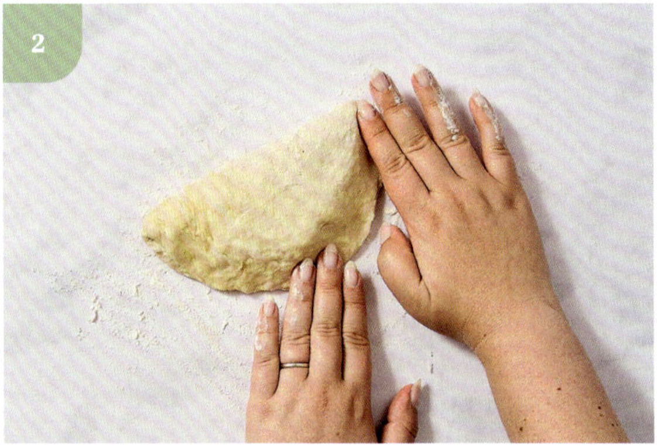

Fold the round in half, pinching the edges together to seal.

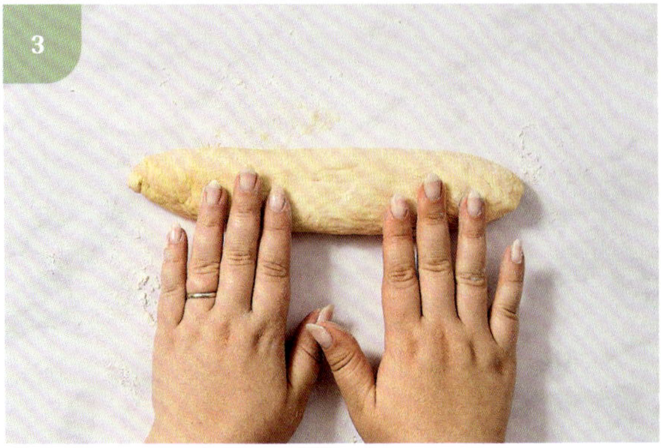

Roll the dough so the pinched seam is against the counter, then roll it with both hands, applying gentle pressure as you move your hands from the center outward, until you have a smooth log of dough about 11 inches long and 2 inches wide with the seam still against the counter.

Make a long slash about ¼ inch deep down the length of the roll. The lame or knife may snag a little as you score the dough—that's okay. If you need to do a few smaller slashes to create the long slash, or to help the slash open up down the length of the roll, it will be just fine.

Recipe Note

You can shape these into 4 pull-apart dinner rolls or slider buns by following the shaping instructions for Honey-Butter Brioche Dinner Rolls (page 101).

POTATO BURGER BUNS

MAKES
2 BUNS

RISING TIME:
1½ HOURS

BAKE TIME:
20 TO 22 MINUTES

When it comes to a classic burger bun, soft, tender potato buns are where it's at. While some recipes use mashed or instant potatoes, I prefer the consistent results you get from potato flour. To create their signature flat-but-domed shape, these rolls spend their final rise under a sheet pan, just like the kaiser roll (page 76)—this forces the dough to rise outward, rather than upward, giving them the perfect shape for your favorite burger patties!

DOUGH

100g (¾ cup + 4 teaspoons) all-purpose flour

20g (2 tablespoons) potato flour

5g (1¼ teaspoons) sugar

3g (1 teaspoon) Diamond Crystal kosher salt

3g (1 teaspoon) instant yeast

90g (¼ cup + 2 tablespoons) whole milk, *warmed* (90°F)

14g (1 tablespoon) unsalted butter, *melted*

Cooking spray

TOPPING

Egg wash: 1 large egg, *beaten well*

1 teaspoon sesame seeds or poppy seeds (optional)

1. **Mix.** In a medium bowl, whisk together the dry ingredients. Make a well and add the warm milk and melted butter. Use a dough whisk or a fork to mix until the water is incorporated and the dough comes together in one slightly dry mass. Switch to a bowl scraper or your hand and fold the dough over itself in the bowl until it comes together and there are no dry bits left.

2. **Knead.** Turn the dough out onto an unfloured surface and knead until smooth and slightly tacky to the touch, about 2 minutes. Resist adding additional flour unless necessary.

3. **First rise.** Shape the dough into a ball, return it to the bowl, cover, and let rest somewhere warm until the dough passes the Fingerprint Test (page 20), 1 to 1½ hours.

4. **Shape.** Divide the dough in half using a bench scraper (each piece should weigh about 116 grams). Shape each piece of dough into a small, tight ball (see page 34).

5. **Second rise.** Line a sheet pan with parchment paper. Place the shaped rolls on the prepared pan. Spray the tops lightly with cooking spray, then cover with plastic wrap. Place another sheet pan on top of them and gently press down until the bottom of the sheet pan barely reaches the top rim of the pan underneath. Let the buns rise in a warm spot (with the sheet pan on top) until they are puffy and spring back when you poke them, 45 minutes to 1 hour.

6. **Preheat.** Toward the end of the rise time, preheat the oven to 350°F.

7. **Top and bake.** Immediately before baking, brush the buns all over with the egg wash. Sprinkle with sesame or poppy seeds (if using). Bake until shiny and golden brown on top, 20 to 24 minutes. Transfer the buns to a wire rack and let cool completely before slicing.

JUST TWO BAGELS

MAKES
2 BAGELS

RISING TIME:
1 HOUR 10 MINUTES

BAKE TIME:
18 TO 20 MINUTES

People are *so* scared to try making bagels from scratch, but once you give this easy recipe a try, you'll be hooked. Bagels are made from a low-hydration dough that's fun to work with, and while this isn't a "traditional" bagel recipe that uses barley malt syrup and bread flour, it's great for beginners. When you see how the dough transforms after boiling and baking it'll feel like you've done a magic trick! Just in time for breakfast, too.

120g (1 cup)
all-purpose flour
+ more for dusting

4g (1 teaspoon)
sugar

3g (1 teaspoon)
Diamond Crystal
kosher salt

1g (heaping ¼ teaspoon)
instant yeast

72g (¼ cup +
2¼ teaspoons)
warm water (90°F)

Cooking spray

Egg wash: 1 large egg,
beaten well

2 tablespoons bagel toppings (optional), such as everything bagel seasoning, sesame seeds, poppy seeds, dried minced onion, etc.

1. **Mix.** In a medium bowl, whisk together the dry ingredients. Make a well in the center and add the warm water. Use a dough whisk or a fork to mix until the water is incorporated and the dough comes together in one shaggy mass, then switch to a bowl scraper or your hand and fold the dough over itself just until it comes together. There might be a few dry bits left in the bowl and that's okay.

2. **Knead.** On a lightly floured surface, knead the dough until smooth and slightly tacky to the touch, 5 to 6 minutes. Lightly dust with flour only as needed, just to prevent sticking.

3. **First rise.** Lightly grease the bowl with cooking spray. Shape the dough into a ball, return it to the greased bowl, cover, and let it rest somewhere warm until it doubles in size and passes the Fingerprint Test (page 20), 1 to 1½ hours.

4. **Preheat.** Toward the end of the rise time, line a sheet pan with parchment paper and preheat the oven to 425°F. Fill a wide medium pot with at least 2 inches of water and bring to a low boil.

5. **Shape.** While the water comes to a boil, divide the dough in half using a bench scraper (each half should weigh about 100 grams). Shape each half into a tight ball (see page 34). Shape the bagels following the instructions in photos 1 and 2.

6. **Second rise.** Place the bagels on the prepared sheet pan, cover with a damp paper towel, and let them rest for 10 minutes.

7. **Boil.** Give each bagel a quick final stretch following the same technique from photo 2 (to prevent the holes from closing up). Place the bagels in the water, top-side down. Boil for 1 minute, then use a spider skimmer to flip them and boil for 1 minute more. Use the spider skimmer to remove the bagels from the pot and slide them back onto the parchment-lined sheet pan.

8. **Bake.** Brush the bagels lightly with the egg wash and sprinkle with any desired toppings. Bake until golden brown and shiny on top, 18 to 20 minutes. Transfer to a wire rack and let cool slightly before eating.

Recipe Note

Boiling is a *crucial* step in the bagel-making process (and for many pretzel recipes, too–see page 88). The hot water gelatinizes the starches in the crust, setting them in place. It prevents the bagels from expanding too much in the oven and gives the crust its signature smooth, shiny texture. Remember: *If they're not boiled, they're not bagels!*

Push your thumb gently through the pinched-together seam at the bottom of the dough ball. (This pushes all those edges together and gives the bagel a cleaner, neater look.)

Gently insert your other thumb and begin squeezing and stretching as you rotate the bagel in your hands to gradually widen the hole until it's about 2 inches across.

BAGEL FLAVORS AND VARIATIONS

- **Asiago:** Add 10 grams of finely grated Asiago cheese to the dough in step 1. Top the bagels with more grated Asiago after applying the egg wash in step 8.
- **Everything bagel:** Add 1 teaspoon everything bagel seasoning to the dough in step 1 and top each bagel with more everything bagel seasoning in step 8.
- **Onion:** Add 5 to 10 grams of finely minced raw onion to the dough in step 1 and top each bagel with dried minced onion in step 8. (You may need to add more flour during kneading to account for the moisture from the onions.)
- **Mini bagels:** Divide the dough into 4 pieces in step 5, boil for only 30 seconds per side, and reduce the bake time to 15 minutes.

JUST TWO
BAGELS

SOFT PRETZEL BUNS

SOFT PRETZEL BUNS

MAKES 2 BUNS

RISING TIME:
1½ HOURS

BAKE TIME:
15 TO 17 MINUTES

If you love pretzels but wish they were a bit more burger- or sandwich-friendly, these pretzel buns are for you. They're super soft and squishy but have that distinctive burnished brown, shiny pretzel crust thanks to a quick dip in a baking soda bath before baking. I love using these for smashburgers, but they're also great for deli sandwiches with plenty of mustard!

DOUGH

120g (1 cup) all-purpose flour + more for dusting

4g (1 teaspoon tightly packed) brown sugar

3g (1 teaspoon) instant yeast

2g (heaping ½ teaspoon) Diamond Crystal kosher salt

70g (¼ cup + 2 teaspoons) warm water (90°F)

14g (1 tablespoon) unsalted butter, *melted*

Cooking spray

BOILING SOLUTION

About 5 cups water

⅓ cup baking soda

TOPPING

Egg wash: 1 large egg, *beaten well*

½ teaspoon pretzel salt

1. **Mix.** In a medium bowl, whisk together the dry ingredients. Make a well in the center and add the warm water and melted butter. Use a dough whisk or a fork to mix until the water is incorporated and the dough comes together in one shaggy mass with a few dry patches. Switch to a bench scraper or your hand and fold the dough over itself until it comes together and there are no dry bits left.

2. **Knead.** Turn the dough out onto a lightly floured surface and knead until smooth and slightly tacky to the touch, about 2 minutes. Resist dusting in more flour unless necessary.

3. **First rise.** Lightly grease the bowl with cooking spray. Shape the dough into a ball, return it to the greased bowl, cover, and let rest somewhere warm until the dough passes the Fingerprint Test (page 20), 1 to 1½ hours.

4. **Shape.** Divide the dough in half using a bench scraper (each piece should weigh about 107 grams). Shape each piece into a tight ball (see page 34).

5. **Second rise.** Line a sheet pan with parchment paper. Place the pretzel buns on the prepared pan and cover them loosely with a kitchen towel. Let them rest for 10 minutes, then give each bun a quick scoot under a cupped palm on an unfloured counter to tighten them up again. Place the buns back on the pan, cover with the towel, and let rise until slightly puffy, 20 to 30 minutes.

6. **Preheat.** Toward the end of the rise time, preheat the oven to 400°F.

7. **Prepare the boiling solution.** Fill a medium pot with at least 2 inches of water (about 5 cups). Stir in the baking soda and bring to a low boil.

8. **Boil the buns.** When the buns are ready, reduce the water to a gentle simmer. Follow the instructions in photos 1 and 2 to boil the buns.

9. **Top and bake.** Immediately before baking, brush the buns with the egg wash, sprinkle with pretzel salt, and score following the instructions in photo 3. Bake until deeply browned, 15 to 17 minutes. Transfer the buns to a wire rack to cool completely before slicing.

Recipe Note

You can divide this dough into thirds or quarters to make dinner rolls or slider buns! The boiling time will remain the same, while the baking time may be a few minutes less.

Place the buns in the water, top-side down, for 30 seconds. Use a spider skimmer or slotted spoon to periodically submerge the buns so the bottoms boil, too.

Use the spider skimmer to flip the buns over in the pot, lift them from the water, then slide them back onto the parchment-lined sheet pan.

Sprinkle the top of each egg-washed bun with pretzel salt. Use a lame or a sharp knife to score an X about ¼ inch deep in the top of each bun.

ONION AND POPPY SEED BIALYS

MAKES 2 BIALYS

RISING TIME:
1½ HOURS

BAKE TIME:
17 TO 20 MINUTES

DOUGH

120g (1 cup) all-purpose flour + more for dusting

3g (1 teaspoon) Diamond Crystal kosher salt

1g (heaping ¼ teaspoon) instant yeast

75g (¼ cup + 1 tablespoon) warm water (90°F)

Cooking spray

FILLING

6g (1½ teaspoons) olive oil

20g (2 tablespoons) minced yellow or white onion

⅛ teaspoon garlic powder

Pinch of salt

Pinch of ground black pepper

½ teaspoon poppy seeds

Originating in Białystok, Poland, bialys are round buns with a divot in the center filled with a savory onion-garlic-poppy-seed filling. They're a distant cousin of the bagel and, like bagels, are made with a low-hydration dough and often served with cream cheese, capers, and lox. Unlike bagels, however, they don't have a hole, they don't have any sugar in the dough, and they aren't boiled before baking.

1. Mix. In a medium bowl, whisk together the dry ingredients. Make a well in the center and add the warm water. Use a dough whisk or a fork to mix until the water is incorporated and the dough comes together in one shaggy mass with just a few dry bits, then switch to a bowl scraper or your hand and fold the dough over itself until it comes together. There might be a few dry bits left in the bowl and that's okay.

2. Knead. On a lightly floured surface, knead the dough until smooth and slightly tacky to the touch, 2 to 3 minutes (lightly dust with more flour just to prevent sticking).

3. First rise. Lightly grease the bowl with cooking spray. Shape the dough into a ball, return it to the greased bowl, cover, and let rest somewhere warm until it doubles in size and passes the Fingerprint Test (page 20), 1 to 1½ hours.

4. Make the filling. In a small skillet, heat the oil over medium heat. Add the minced onion, garlic powder, salt, and pepper. Cook, stirring frequently, until the onions are soft and translucent, about 5 minutes. Stir in the poppy seeds and cook for 30 seconds more. Set aside to cool.

5. Preshape. Divide the dough in half using a bench scraper (each piece should weigh about 100 grams). Shape each half into a tight ball (see page 34) and place seam-side down on the counter.

6. Second rise. Dust the tops of the balls with flour and cover them with a clean kitchen towel. Let them rise until slightly puffy and the seams underneath have sealed shut, about 30 minutes.

7. Preheat. Toward the end of the rise time, preheat the oven to 450°F. Line a sheet pan with parchment paper.

8. Shape. Dust each ball generously with flour on both sides. Follow the instructions in photos 1 and 2 to shape one bialy. Set the first bialy down on the prepared sheet pan while you shape the second. The dough will shrink back slightly as it rests. Finish by repeating the stretching process in photo 2 quickly on each bialy.

9. Bake. Divide the filling evenly between the bialys, spooning it into the center and then spreading it up the sides of the crater you've made in the dough. Bake until pale brown around the edges, 17 to 20 minutes. Transfer the bialys to a wire rack and let them cool slightly before eating. (The bialys will be firm to the touch when they first come out of the oven but will soften as they cool.)

Recipe Notes

- If at any point during the shaping process the dough is fighting you, or feels like it's tearing, or doesn't want to stretch, let it rest for a few minutes. This lets the gluten relax so you can resume stretching.
- If you accidentally tear through the center of a bialy, just pinch the dough back together. Let it rest for just a few minutes, then try stretching it again.

Use the pads of your thumbs to gently press down in the center of the ball of dough until you can feel your fingertips on the other side. Do not poke through the middle.

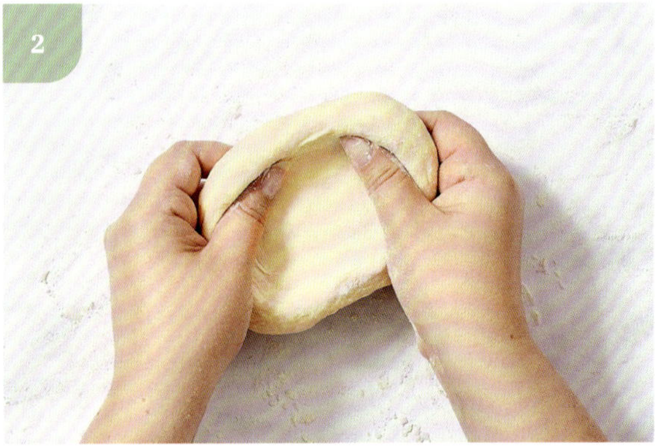

Stretch the divot by rotating the dough through your hands. Bring your thumbs together, then slide them away from each other about an inch or so, tugging lightly on the center of the dough. Keep going until the bialy is about 5 inches across (the rim should be about 1 inch wide and the divot about 3 inches wide).

ONION AND POPPY SEED BIALYS

STOVETOP
ENGLISH MUFFINS

STOVETOP ENGLISH MUFFINS

MAKES
3 ENGLISH MUFFINS

RISING TIME:
2 HOURS

COOK TIME:
8 TO 10 MINUTES

120g (1 cup)
all-purpose flour

5g (1¼ teaspoons)
sugar

5g (1 teaspoon +
heaping ½ teaspoon)
Diamond Crystal
kosher salt

3g (1 teaspoon)
instant yeast

4g (1 teaspoon)
baking powder

70g (¼ cup
+ 2 teaspoons)
warm water (90°F)

14g (1 tablespoon)
unsalted butter, *melted*

Olive oil (for the
bowl and pan)

1 tablespoon semolina
flour + more if you
need it (for coating)

These soft, buttery English muffins are inspired by the homemade English muffins that I get at Mike & Patty's, a local breakfast shop here in Boston. They are super soft and a little more bready inside than a grocery store English muffin, but I think that makes them a perfect base for eggs Benedict or your favorite breakfast sandwich. While some English muffin recipes call for cornmeal on the outside, I prefer the finer grain of semolina flour. No oven needed here—English muffins cook right on the stovetop!

1. Mix. In a medium bowl, whisk together the flour, sugar, salt, yeast, and baking powder. Make a well in the center and add the warm water and melted butter. Use a dough whisk or a fork to mix until the water is incorporated and the dough comes together in one shaggy mass, then use a bowl scraper or your hand to fold the dough over itself until it comes together and there are no dry bits left.

2. Knead. Turn the dough out onto an unfloured surface and knead until smooth and slightly tacky to the touch, 2 to 4 minutes (the dough will feel rough and a little wet at first but will smooth out as you knead). Resist adding flour unless necessary.

3. First rise. Lightly oil the bowl. Shape the dough into a ball, return it to the greased bowl, cover, and let rest somewhere warm until the dough doubles in size and passes the Fingerprint Test (page 20), 1 to 1½ hours.

4. Shape. Divide the dough into 3 equal portions using a bench scraper (each piece should weigh about 72 grams). Shape each piece of dough into a tight ball (see page 34).

5. Shape and second rise. Line a sheet pan with parchment paper. Sprinkle the parchment with half of the semolina flour and place the dough balls on the prepared pan. Shape the English muffins and prep them for their second rise following the instructions in photos 1 and 2. Let the English muffins rise in a warm spot with the sheet pan on top of them until they've about doubled in size (about 3 inches across), 1 to 1½ hours (photo 3).

6. **Preheat the skillet.** Preheat a dry 10-inch cast-iron or stainless steel skillet over medium heat. When drops of water flicked onto the surface of the pan sizzle and evaporate immediately, add 2 tablespoons olive oil and swirl to coat the surface of the pan.

7. **Cook.** Reduce the heat to slightly below medium and arrange the English muffins in the pan. Cook, flipping every 2 to 3 minutes, until they're well browned on the outside and reach an internal temperature of 190° to 200°F, 6 to 12 minutes total (photo 4). Press down lightly on each muffin once after flipping and rotate the muffins in place periodically so they brown evenly. Adjust the heat and add more oil to the pan as needed to prevent burning. Transfer the English muffins to a wire rack and let cool slightly before eating.

Recipe Notes

- You can do most of the prep work the night before and enjoy English muffins in the morning! Place the shaped English muffins in the fridge with the sheet pan weighting them down on top and let them rise overnight. Pull the sheet pan out of the fridge and let rest for 1 hour at room temperature with the sheet pan still on top before cooking.

- To get that classic craggy English muffin texture inside, use a fork to poke holes close together all the way around the circumference of the English muffin until it splits.

recipe continues

1

Place the dough balls on the sheet pan, with the seam side facing down. Sprinkle the tops with the remaining semolina flour, then press down gently on the top of each one.

2

Cover the English muffins with plastic wrap, then place another sheet pan on top to weight them down as they rise. Press down gently until the bottom of the sheet pan meets the top rim of the pan underneath.

3

Let the English muffins rise in a warm spot with the sheet pan on top until they're about doubled in size (about 3 inches across), 1 to 1½ hours. They should look quite airy and spring back slightly when you poke them.

4

You might hear a very gentle sizzling, but won't see much spattering in the pan. Press down lightly on top of each muffin just once immediately after flipping.

RESTAURANT-STYLE FRENCH DINNER ROLLS

MAKES
4 DINNER ROLLS

RISING TIME:
1 HOUR 45 MINUTES

BAKE TIME:
13 TO 15 MINUTES

These crusty French dinner rolls are just like the ones you get tucked inside the bread basket at mid-tier dressy-casual restaurants. This is another relatively low-hydration dough that's a lot of fun to work with. It bakes up into rolls that are soft inside with a thin, crispy crust that crackles around your fingertips when you break into it. Perfect for tearing into chunks and spreading with a pat of salted butter or dunking in your favorite soups!

120g (1 cup)
all-purpose flour
+ more for dusting

2g (½ teaspoon)
sugar

2g (heaping
½ teaspoon)
Diamond Crystal
kosher salt

1g (heaping
¼ teaspoon)
instant yeast

80g (⅓ cup)
warm water (90°F)

Cooking spray

1. **Mix.** In a medium bowl, whisk together the dry ingredients. Make a well in the center and add the warm water. Use a dough whisk or a fork to mix until the water is incorporated and the dough comes together in one shaggy mass, then use a bench scraper or your hand to fold the dough over itself until there are no dry bits left.

2. **Knead.** Turn the dough out onto a lightly floured surface and knead until smooth and slightly tacky to the touch, about 2 minutes. Dust in additional flour lightly only as needed.

3. **First rise.** Shape the dough into a ball, place it in a bowl, cover, and let rest somewhere warm until it's slightly puffy and passes the Fingerprint Test (page 20), 1 to 1½ hours. The dough may not fully double in size, but it should look larger.

4. **Shape.** Divide the dough into 4 equal portions using a bench scraper (each piece should weigh about 51 grams). Shape each piece into a tight ball (see page 34), then shape each ball into a roll, following the instructions in photo 1.

5. **Second rise.** Line a sheet pan with parchment paper. Place the shaped rolls on the prepared pan. Dust them lightly with flour, spray the tops lightly with cooking spray, and cover loosely with plastic wrap. Let them rise at room temperature until they spring back when you poke them, 30 to 45 minutes.

6. **Preheat.** Toward the end of the rise time, preheat the oven to 450°F and fill a small spray bottle or bowl with water.

7. **Bake.** Immediately before baking, wet and score the rolls as shown in photo 2. Bake until pale golden brown on top, 13 to 15 minutes. Transfer the rolls to a wire rack and let cool almost completely before serving—these are best served slightly warm!

Recipe Note

If you have a perforated baguette baking pan, you can let the rolls do their second rise and bake in that pan for an extra-crisp crust.

With the seam against the counter, briefly press down on the middle of each dough ball and roll it back and forth with gentle yet firm pressure to shape it into a short oval, about 3 inches long and 1½ inches wide.

Spritz or brush the rolls generously with water. Score a ¼-inch-deep slash down the center of each roll. Make sure the score mark goes end-to-end for the best results.

HONEY~BUTTER BRIOCHE DINNER ROLLS

MAKES
4 DINNER ROLLS

RISING TIME:
1½ HOURS

BAKE TIME:
16 TO 18 MINUTES

DOUGH

Dough from Classic Brioche Loaf (page 65)

Unsalted butter (for greasing)

TO FINISH

Egg wash: 1 large egg, *beaten well*

¼ teaspoon flaky sea salt

14g (1 tablespoon) unsalted butter, *melted and cooled slightly*

7g (1 teaspoon) honey

These honey-butter dinner rolls showcase just how versatile brioche dough can be. Instead of baking a single loaf, the dough is divided and shaped into adorably petite dinner rolls. They're topped with flaky salt and melted honey butter—that salty-sweet finish combined with the soft, fluffy rolls is well worth the effort!

1. **Mix and rise.** Make the brioche dough as directed through the first rise (step 5).

2. **Shape.** Divide the dough into 4 equal portions using a bench scraper (each piece should weigh about 54 grams). Shape each piece of dough into a tight ball (see page 34).

3. **Second rise.** Butter a 5- or 6-inch square baking dish and arrange the shaped rolls inside. Cover loosely with plastic wrap and let the rolls rise in a warm spot until they're doubled in size and quite puffy, 1 to 1½ hours. (If your kitchen is cold, the rolls may not visibly expand much—that's okay.)

4. **Preheat.** Toward the end of the rise time, preheat the oven to 350°F.

5. **Bake.** Immediately before baking, brush the rolls with the egg wash and sprinkle each roll with a *tiny* pinch of flaky salt. Bake until shiny and golden brown on top, 16 to 18 minutes.

6. **Top.** While the rolls bake, whisk together the melted butter and honey. Brush the honey butter all over the rolls immediately after removing them from the oven (keep them in the pan!). Let the rolls cool for 10 minutes in the pan, then transfer to a wire rack to cool almost completely before serving. These rolls are best served slightly warm.

VARIATIONS

- **Brioche Slider Buns:** Skip the honey-butter topping.
- **Garlic Butter Brioche Rolls:** Add ¼ teaspoon garlic powder to the dry ingredients in step 1 and brush with the garlic butter topping from the "Limited" Garlic Breadsticks (page 112).

JUST~LIKE~THE~TUBE BUTTERY CRESCENT ROLLS

MAKES
8 CRESCENT ROLLS

RISING TIME:
1 HOUR 40 MINUTES

BAKE TIME:
18 TO 22 MINUTES

To give these buttery crescent rolls a hint of croissant-like flakiness, this dough is best handled while cold. Using warm milk and melted butter in the initial dough mix gives the yeast a jump start, but from then on, you'll want to think of it like a biscuit or pie dough and keep it cold, cold, *cold*. Kneading in the frozen grated butter can get a little messy, but it's totally worth it for those buttery, flaky layers.

DOUGH

14g (1 tablespoon) unsalted butter, *cold from the fridge*

120g (1 cup) all-purpose flour + more for dusting

5g (1 teaspoon + heaping ½ teaspoon) Diamond Crystal kosher salt

4g (1 teaspoon) sugar

3g (1 teaspoon) instant yeast

72g (¼ cup + 2¼ teaspoons) whole milk, *warmed* (90°F)

28g (2 tablespoons) unsalted butter, *melted*

TOPPING

28g (2 tablespoons) unsalted butter, *melted*

Pinch of flaky sea salt (optional)

1. **Prep the butter.** Grate the cold butter on the large holes of a box grater. Set in a small bowl and put in the freezer for at least 10 minutes.

2. **Mix the dough.** In a medium bowl, whisk together the dry ingredients. In a liquid measuring cup, whisk together the warm milk and the melted butter. Add the wet ingredients to the dry ingredients. Use a dough whisk or a fork to mix until the milk is incorporated and the dough mostly comes together. Switch to a bowl scraper or your hand and fold the dough over itself until there are no dry bits left.

3. **Knead.** Knead the dough on a lightly floured surface until smooth and slightly tacky to the touch, about 2 minutes. Shape the dough into a ball.

4. **Chill.** Return the dough to the bowl, cover, and place in the fridge to chill for 10 minutes.

5. **Knead again.** Turn the chilled dough out onto a lightly floured surface. Press it into a flat disc about ½ inch thick. Sprinkle the chilled grated butter over the dough, then fold in the edges to tuck the butter inside (photo 1). Knead the dough briefly with a light touch, just for 30 to 60 seconds (lightly dust with flour as needed). The dough will get a little sticky and slippery, but you don't want the butter to melt completely—you should still see bits of butter in the dough. Shape the dough into a ball to finish.

6. **First rest.** Return the dough to the bowl, cover, and let rest for at least 1 hour or up to overnight in the fridge. It won't rise much or even look much different, but the flour will be hydrated and the gluten relaxed.

7. **Shape.** Turn the dough out onto a lightly floured surface. Lightly flour the top of the dough, too. Roll the dough into an 8-inch round about ¼ inch thick.

recipe continues

Use a bench scraper or a sharp knife to divide the dough into 8 equal wedges (like a pizza). Follow the instructions in photos 2 through 4 to shape the crescents.

8. Second rest. Line a sheet pan with parchment paper. Place the shaped crescent rolls on the prepared pan, cover, and let rest in the fridge for at least 30 minutes or up to overnight.

9. Preheat. Toward the end of the rest time, preheat the oven to 375°F.

10. Top and bake. Brush the tops of the crescent rolls with half of the melted butter. If desired, also sprinkle each roll with a *tiny* pinch of flaky salt. Bake until pale golden brown, 18 to 22 minutes. Remove the rolls from the oven and immediately brush with the remaining melted butter. Let the rolls cool almost completely on a wire rack. These rolls are best served while slightly warm.

VARIATIONS

- **Pigs in a Blanket:** Divide the dough into 16 wedges instead of 8. Place a small cocktail wiener at the short end of the wedge and roll it up toward the narrowest point so the narrow point is tucked underneath and held in place. Check them after 15 minutes in the oven, though they may need the full bake time.

- **Chocolate Croissants:** Roll the dough into a rectangle about ⅛ inch thick. Cut the dough into 4 rectangles. Place a line of chocolate chips about ¼ inch in and parallel to the short ends of each rectangle. Fold the dough over the line of chocolate chips and roll the two ends to meet each other in the middle like a scroll, then flip the croissant over so the smooth side is on top.

- **Ham and Cheese Croissants:** Place a pinch of shredded gruyere or Swiss cheese and a small piece of smoked deli ham at the wide part of the triangle and roll it up inside the crescent dough. Top with more shredded cheese before baking.

Recipe Note

The joined ends of the crescent roll might separate in the oven, giving the rolls a true crescent shape. For log-shaped rolls, don't join the ends as shown in photo 4.

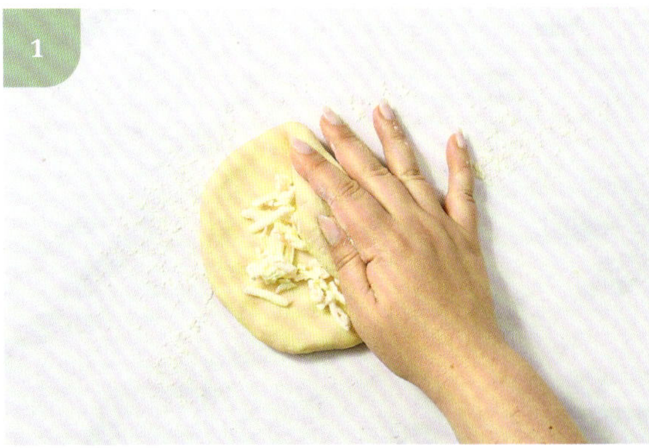

Fold the edges of the dough around the grated butter before kneading. This helps contain the mess as you begin working the dough.

Roll from the center of each wedge out to either end, making each wedge slightly longer and thinner.

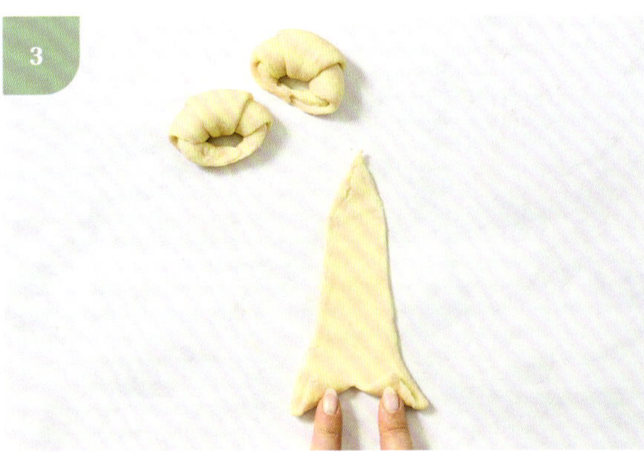

Cut a ½-inch notch in the middle of the shortest side of the wedge, then roll up the dough by first folding up the inner corners of the notch away from one another.

With the point of the wedge on the bottom, bring the two arms of the rolled dough together and pinch to seal.

CHAPTER 3

STICKS, TWISTS, AND BRAIDS

THIN AND CRISPY SESAME BREADSTICKS (GRISSINI)

MAKES
18 BREADSTICKS

RISING TIME:
1½ HOURS

BAKE TIME:
20 TO 22 MINUTES

DOUGH

120g (1 cup)
all-purpose flour
+ more for dusting

3g (1 teaspoon)
Diamond Crystal
kosher salt

3g (1 teaspoon)
instant yeast

75g (¼ cup
+ 1 tablespoon)
warm water (90°F)

4g (1 teaspoon)
olive oil or toasted
sesame oil + more
for greasing

TOPPING

1 tablespoon
sesame seeds

These gangly sesame breadsticks are my take on *grissini* (Italian for "breadsticks"). They're a fabulous addition to your charcuterie boards or antipasti platters (or, *ahem*, girl dinners), though some people prefer eating them with salad and eggs. With just 1 cup of flour, you can make 18 crisp, snappy breadsticks, so this might be the only recipe in the entire book where you find yourself having some left for later.

Sesame seeds are a traditional topping, but you can also use everything bagel seasoning, flaky salt, poppy seeds, shelled sunflower seeds, and so much more.

1. Mix. In a medium bowl, whisk together the dry ingredients. Make a well in the center and add the warm water and olive oil. Use a dough whisk or a fork to mix until the water is absorbed, then use a bowl scraper or your hand to fold the dough over itself in the bowl until it comes together.

2. Knead. Turn the dough out onto a lightly floured counter and knead with a light touch until it smooths out, 2 to 3 minutes. At first, the dough will feel very rough and sticky, bordering on wet, but it will get smoother as you knead. After a couple of minutes it might still have a bit of texture to it—that's fine, but it shouldn't feel sticky or clingy. Add more flour only if you really need it to prevent sticking.

3. Rest. Invert the bowl over the dough on the counter and let it rest at room temperature for 5 minutes. (This allows the gluten to relax and the flour to more fully hydrate.)

4. Knead again. Knead the dough again for about 2 minutes. You will feel it become much smoother and more supple very quickly. Do not add more flour at this stage.

5. First rise. Lightly oil the bowl. Place the dough in the greased bowl, cover, and let it rise until it doubles in size and passes the Fingerprint Test (page 20), 1 to 1½ hours.

6. Add the seed topping. On a clean surface, spoon the sesame seeds into an even layer roughly the size of your dough ball. Turn the dough out of the bowl and place it on top of the seeds. Flip the dough over and use the other side to pick up any additional seeds.

7. Shape. Use your hands and a rolling pin to press, stretch, and roll the dough into a roughly 9 by 7-inch rectangle. Line a sheet pan with parchment paper. Cut and stretch 18 breadsticks following the instructions in photos 1 and 2.

8. Second rise. Cover the pan with plastic wrap and let the breadsticks rise in a warm spot until they look just a little puffy (though they may not look much different at all), 30 to 45 minutes.

9. Preheat. Toward the end of the rise time, preheat the oven to 375°F.

10. Bake. Bake the breadsticks until pale golden brown and hard to the touch, 20 to 22 minutes. They may have some darker brown spots where the breadsticks are at their thinnest. Let cool completely on the sheet pan before eating so they're nice and crispy!

Use a bench scraper or a sharp knife to cut the dough into eighteen ½-inch strips, cutting the short way.

Pick up and stretch each piece of dough until it's 11 to 12 inches long, placing it onto the parchment-lined pan as you stretch. Leave about ½ inch between breadsticks.

THIN AND CRISPY
SESAME BREADSTICKS

"LIMITED" GARLIC
BREADSTICKS

"LIMITED" GARLIC BREADSTICKS

MAKES
4 BREADSTICKS

RISING TIME:
1½ HOURS

BAKE TIME:
18 TO 22 MINUTES

Okay, sure, just four buttery, garlicky breadsticks might not be the same *unlimited* option you're used to at the garden of olives, but these are perfect for serving alongside a big bowl of spaghetti for one (or two!).

High-protein/high-gluten bread flour provides the strength and structure needed for the breadsticks to hold their shape, but all-purpose flour will work fine if that's all you've got.

GARLIC SALT

6g (2 teaspoons) Diamond Crystal kosher salt

4g (1 teaspoon) garlic powder

DOUGH

120g (1 cup) bread flour + more for dusting

6g (2 teaspoons) garlic salt, from above

4g (1 teaspoon) sugar

3g (1 teaspoon) instant yeast

72g (¼ cup + 2¼ teaspoons) warm water (90°F)

14g (1 tablespoon) unsalted butter, *melted*

Cooking spray

1. **Make the garlic salt.** In a small bowl, mix the salt and garlic powder until well combined.

2. **Mix the dough.** In a medium bowl, whisk together the dry ingredients. Make a well in the center and add the warm water and melted butter. Use a dough whisk or a fork to mix the dough until all the water is absorbed, then use a bowl scraper or your hand to fold the dough over itself in the bowl until it comes together.

3. **Knead.** Turn the dough out onto a lightly floured surface and knead until smooth and slightly tacky to the touch, 2 to 3 minutes. The dough will feel rough and a little sticky at first but will smooth out as you knead. Lightly dust more flour onto the counter only as needed to prevent sticking.

4. **Rest.** Invert the bowl over the dough on the counter and let it rest at room temperature for 10 minutes. (This allows the gluten to relax and the flour to fully hydrate.)

5. **Knead again.** Knead the dough again for 20 to 30 seconds—you will feel it become much smoother and more supple very quickly as you knead. Do not add more flour at this stage.

6. **First rise.** Grease the bowl with cooking spray. Place the dough in the greased bowl, cover, and let rise until it doubles in size and passes the Fingerprint Test (page 20), about 1 hour.

7. **Shape.** Gently deflate the dough with your fingertips and divide it into 4 equal portions using a bench scraper (each piece should weigh about 54 grams). Roll each piece of dough into a log following the instructions in photo 1.

TOPPING

14g (1 tablespoon) unsalted butter, *melted*

Remaining garlic salt

Dried oregano, basil, and/or parsley (optional)

Finely grated Parmesan or Pecorino Romano cheese (optional)

8. Second rise. Line a sheet pan with parchment paper. Arrange the 4 breadsticks on the prepared pan, about ½ inch apart. Spray the top of the breadsticks lightly with cooking spray, cover loosely with plastic wrap, and let them rise in a warm spot until they just about double in size and spring back when you poke them, 30 to 45 minutes.

9. Preheat. Toward the end of the rise time, preheat the oven to 400°F.

10. Top. Immediately before baking, brush about half the melted butter generously over the breadsticks (photo 2) and sprinkle with the remaining garlic salt.

11. Bake. Bake until the breadsticks are golden brown on top, 18 to 22 minutes. Remove from the oven and immediately brush with the remaining melted butter and sprinkle with any additional toppings desired. Transfer to a wire rack and let cool slightly before serving. Garlic breadsticks are best served warm!

Gently roll each piece into a rope about 5 inches long. Then, starting with the first rope you rolled, roll each rope to about 8 inches long. The dough will shrink back slightly, so I find it helps to roll each rope to about 10 inches and let it shrink back to 8 inches.

Use a light touch with the pastry brush so you don't deflate the breadsticks. Make sure to get butter on the sides of the breadsticks, too.

ONE LARGE SOFT PRETZEL

MAKES
1 LARGE PRETZEL

RISING TIME:
1 HOUR 10 MINUTES

BAKE TIME:
10 TO 12 MINUTES

Though pretzels traditionally get their dark brown color and signature pretzel flavor from a quick bath in food-grade lye, we're keeping things simple (and safer) by quickly boiling this single large soft pretzel in a simple baking soda solution instead. Just as when making bagels (see page 84), boiling helps gelatinize the starches in the crust, producing a shiny texture and preventing the pretzel from expanding too much during baking.

DOUGH

120g (1 cup) all-purpose flour + more for dusting

4g (1 teaspoon packed) brown sugar

2g (heaping ½ teaspoon) Diamond Crystal kosher salt

1g (heaping ¼ teaspoon) instant yeast

70g (¼ cup + 2 teaspoons) warm water (90°F)

14g (1 tablespoon) unsalted butter, *melted*

BOILING SOLUTION

About 5 cups water

⅓ cup baking soda

TOPPING

Egg wash: 1 large egg, *beaten well*

¼ to ½ teaspoon pretzel salt

1. **Mix.** In a medium bowl, whisk together the dry ingredients. Make a well in the center and add the warm water and melted butter. Use a dough whisk or a fork to mix until the liquid is absorbed and just a bit of loose dry bits remain, then use a bowl scraper or your hand to fold the dough over itself until it comes together.

2. **Knead.** Turn the dough out onto a lightly floured surface and knead until smooth and slightly tacky to the touch, 2 to 3 minutes. Lightly dust more flour onto the dough only as needed to prevent sticking.

3. **Rise.** Shape the dough into a ball, return it to the bowl, cover, and let rest in a warm spot until the dough passes the Fingerprint Test (page 20), 1 to 1½ hours. It may not completely double in size—that's okay.

4. **Preheat.** Toward the end of the rise time, preheat the oven to 450°F. Line a sheet pan with parchment paper.

5. **Prepare the boiling solution.** Fill a medium pot with at least 2 inches of water (about 5 cups). Stir in the baking soda and bring to a low boil.

6. **Shape.** While the water comes to a boil, turn the dough out onto a clean work surface. Gently deflate the dough with your fingertips, pressing it into a rough rectangle shape with one of the long sides closest to you. Roll the top long edge toward you until you have a nice fat log. Moving your hands from the center of the log to the ends, roll the dough into a 34-inch rope, slightly tapering the ends. Shape the dough into a pretzel following the instructions in photos 1 and 2. Transfer the pretzel to the prepared pan.

7. **Rest.** Cover the shaped pretzel with plastic wrap and let it rest for 5 to 10 minutes.

8. **Boil.** Reduce the water to a gentle simmer. Place the pretzel in the water with the top side facing up. Boil for 45 seconds, occasionally using a spider skimmer or a slotted spoon to gently submerge the pretzel. Carefully lift and transfer the pretzel to the prepared sheet pan.

9. **Top and bake.** Brush the egg wash all over the pretzel. Sprinkle with the pretzel salt. Bake until dark brown and shiny on top, 10 to 12 minutes. Transfer to a wire rack and let cool slightly before serving.

Recipe Note

Be gentle when transferring the pretzel in and out of the simmering baking soda solution—you don't want the twisted shape to come apart.

Arrange the rope in a U-shape. Cross the ends over each other. Cross the ends a second time.

Fold the ends down and secure to either side of the curve at the bottom of the U. Press them down gently to seal.

VARIATION

Pretzel Bites: In step 6, roll the dough into a rope 1 to 2 inches thick without tapered ends. Cut the rope into 2-inch pieces. Boil for just 20 seconds and bake for 8 to 10 minutes.

ONE LARGE
SOFT PRETZEL

ULTRACHEESY
GARLIC KNOTS

ULTRACHEESY GARLIC KNOTS

MAKES
6 GARLIC KNOTS

RISING TIME:
2 HOURS

BAKE TIME:
17 TO 20 MINUTES

DOUGH

120g (1 cup) all-purpose flour + more for dusting

5g (1½ tablespoons) finely grated Parmesan cheese

4g (½ teaspoon) Diamond Crystal kosher salt

3g (1 teaspoon) instant yeast

2g (½ teaspoon) garlic powder

70g (¼ cup + 2 teaspoons) warm water (90°F)

7g (1 heaping teaspoon) minced garlic

4g (1 teaspoon) olive oil + a little more for the bowl

Twelve ½-inch cubes low-moisture whole-milk mozzarella cheese

---

GARLIC BUTTER

28g (2 tablespoons) unsalted butter, *melted*

7g (1 teaspoon) minced garlic

⅛ teaspoon garlic powder

Garlic knots are great, but you know what's even better? Garlic knots stuffed with cheese and topped with even more cheese and oh, what the heck, served alongside a big slice of cheesy pizza probably. These garlic knots have an intense garlicky flavor thanks to the combination of minced fresh garlic and garlic powder in the dough *and* in the garlic butter topping, but it's the blend of mozzarella and Parmesan cheeses that gives them that classic pizza parlor flavor.

For the best results, use fresh, finely grated Parmesan cheese, not the stuff from the big plastic canister. And don't worry about making perfect scout-approved knots; they're going to be covered in melty, gloriously browned cheese anyway!

1. **Mix.** In a medium bowl, whisk together the dry ingredients. Make a well in the center and add the warm water, minced garlic, and oil. Use a dough whisk or a fork to mix until the liquid is absorbed and just a few dry bits remain, then use a bowl scraper or your hand to fold the dough over itself until it comes together.

2. **Knead.** Turn the dough out onto a lightly floured surface and knead until smooth and slightly tacky to the touch, about 2 minutes. The dough will feel rough and a little sticky at first but will smooth out as you knead. Add more flour only as needed to prevent sticking.

3. **First rise.** Place the dough in a lightly oiled bowl, cover, and let it rise until it doubles in size and passes the Fingerprint Test (page 20), 1 to 1½ hours.

4. **Shape.** Gently deflate the dough with your fingertips and use a bench scraper to divide it into 6 equal portions (each piece should weigh about 35 grams). Roll each piece into a 7-inch rope. Follow the instructions in photos 1 through 4 to stuff each rope with mozzarella cheese and shape it into a knot.

5. **Second rise.** Line a sheet pan with parchment paper. Arrange the 6 garlic knots on the prepared pan. Cover loosely with plastic wrap and let rise in a warm spot until quite puffy, 45 minutes to 1 hour.

6. **Preheat.** Toward the end of the rise time, preheat the oven to 375°F.

7. **Make the garlic butter.** In a small bowl, stir together the melted butter, minced fresh garlic, and garlic powder.

TOPPING

30g (heaping ¼ cup) shredded low-moisture whole-milk mozzarella cheese

20g (about ⅓ cup) finely grated Parmesan cheese + more to taste (measure with your heart!)

8. Top. Immediately before baking, spoon the garlic butter evenly over the knots. Top each one with a pinch of grated mozzarella and a generous dusting of Parmesan cheese.

9. Bake. Bake the knots until the cheese is browned on top and the visible dough around the sides is pale golden brown, 17 to 20 minutes. Let the knots cool on the pan for at least 10 minutes before serving. These are best enjoyed while still warm!

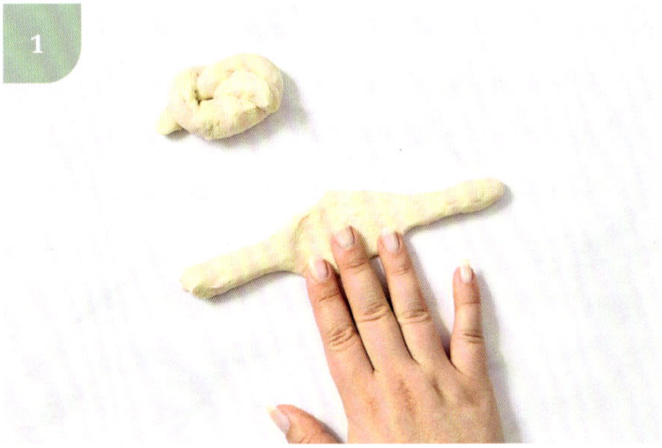

Use a rolling pin or your fingers to flatten a 2- to 3-inch section in the middle of the dough rope.

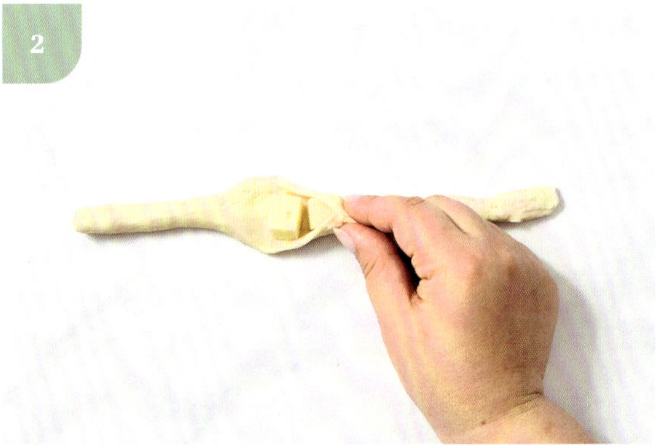

Place 2 cubes of mozzarella cheese on the flattened portion of dough, then stretch and pinch the dough closed around them. Don't worry about making them perfect!

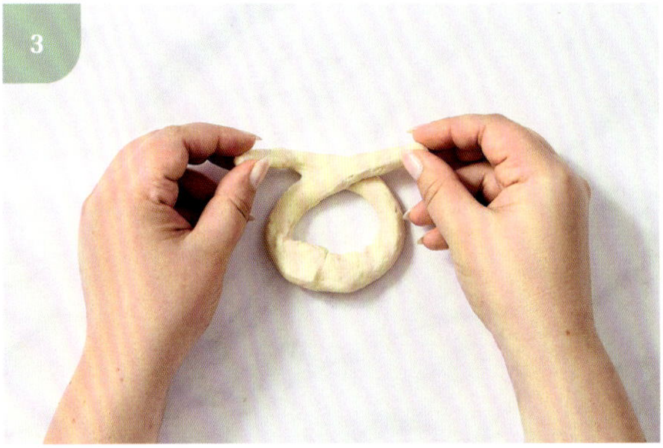

Cross the two ends of the rope over each other to make a loop.

Tuck one end of the rope through the loop to make a knot. Don't worry if your knots seem a little uneven, they will fill out as they rise.

SPARKLING NUTELLA STAR BREAD

MAKES
1 SMALL LOAF

RISING TIME:
1½ HOURS

BAKE TIME:
19 TO 22 MINUTES

Star breads—also known as tartes de soleil—are one of those baking projects that look so much more complicated than they are. This one is made using flaky, buttery crescent roll dough with a generous spread of Nutella twisted inside—it's a perfect pull-apart dessert to enjoy around the holidays.

A sprinkle of coarse-grained ✨sparkling sugar✨ (that's literally what it's called!) adds just the right amount of crunch and sweetness, but if you want to get creative, consider adding a bit of orange zest, chopped nuts, or shredded coconut to the Nutella layer.

P.S. Don't skip chilling the dough before baking—cold butter is what makes this bread extra flaky!

DOUGH

Dough from Just-Like-the-Tube Buttery Crescent Rolls (page 103)

Cooking spray

FILLING

50g (2 tablespoons + 2 teaspoons) Nutella

8g (2 teaspoons) granulated sugar

TOPPING

14g (1 tablespoon) unsalted butter, *melted*

1 teaspoon sparkling sugar

Powdered sugar (optional; for dusting)

1. **Make the dough.** Make the buttery crescent dough as directed through step 5 (Knead Again). Divide the dough in half and shape it into 2 balls (each ball should weigh about 123 grams). Lightly grease the bowl with cooking spray, place the balls inside, cover, and let them rest in the fridge for 1 hour. (They will not grow in size, but this will give the butter time to firm up, the starches time to hydrate, and the gluten network time to relax.)

2. **Prep the filling.** When the hour is up, microwave the Nutella in two to three 10-second bursts, stirring in between, to make it easier to spread.

3. **Shape.** Line a sheet pan with parchment paper. On a lightly floured surface, roll each dough ball into a 7-inch round (about ⅛ inch thick). Dividing evenly, sprinkle each round all over with the granulated sugar. Flip one round onto the prepared sheet pan so the sugar side is facing down. Follow the instructions in photos 1 through 4 to fill and create the star shape.

4. **Chill.** Cover with plastic wrap and place the sheet pan in the fridge for at least 30 minutes or as long as overnight before baking.

5. **Preheat.** Toward the end of the chilling time, preheat the oven to 375°F.

6. **Top and bake.** Brush the top of the star bread with the melted butter, then sprinkle with the sparkling sugar. Bake until light golden brown around the edges, 19 to 22 minutes. Carefully slide the bread onto a wire rack. Let cool for at least 10 minutes. Dust with powdered sugar (if using) before serving.

Use a mini offset spatula or a table knife to spread the warm Nutella over the top of the dough, all the way to the edges. Place the second dough round on top of the Nutella layer, sugar-side up.

Place a 1½-inch bowl or shot glass in the center of the round (DO NOT push down!). Divide the round into quarters with a bench scraper, then divide each quarter in half, then in half again so you have 16 equal-size wedges of dough.

Twist each strip three times, alternating the direction you twist each strip.

Pinch the ends of each pair of strips together to make a point. Repeat all the way around the circle. Brush the ends of the dough with a bit of water to help them stick if you're having trouble.

Ateco
#1385
SOUPER CUBES
SOUPER CUBES

OOEY-GOOEY CINNAMON ROLLS

MAKES
4 ROLLS

RISING TIME:
2½ TO 3½ HOURS

BAKE TIME:
20 TO 22 MINUTES

DOUGH

120g (1 cup)
all-purpose flour
+ more for dusting

3g (1 teaspoon)
Diamond Crystal
kosher salt

3g (1 teaspoon)
instant yeast

21g (1½ tablespoons)
unsalted butter, *melted*

15g (1 heaping tablespoon)
granulated sugar

1 large egg, *at room temperature*

¼ teaspoon
vanilla extract

20g (4 teaspoons)
whole milk, *warmed* (90°F)

Cooking spray

Sometimes you want cinnamon rolls but you don't necessarily want a whole freaking sheet pan of them, you know? That's where this recipe comes in clutch. It makes four petite cinnamon rolls that bake up extra ooey-gooey thanks to a bit of milk poured over them right before they hit the oven. The dough soaks up all that milk as it bakes, making them extra soft and tender.

This recipe uses a quick and easy buttery dough but if you want to get fancy, you can use the brioche dough (page 65) with ¼ teaspoon vanilla added to the wet ingredients instead.

1. **Mix.** In a medium bowl, whisk together the flour, salt, and yeast. In a liquid measuring cup, whisk the melted butter, granulated sugar, egg, vanilla, and warmed milk. Make a well in the center of the dry ingredients and add the milk mixture. Use a dough whisk or a fork to mix until the dough forms large clumps, then use a bowl scraper or your hand to fold the dough over itself in the bowl until it comes together.

2. **Knead.** Turn the dough onto a floured surface and knead until smooth and slightly tacky to the touch, 2 to 3 minutes, dusting in additional flour lightly as needed. Shape the dough into a ball.

3. **First rise.** Lightly grease the bowl with cooking spray, place the dough ball inside, cover, and set aside to rise at room temperature until the dough puffs up and passes the Fingerprint Test (page 20), 1 to 1½ hours (it may not fully double in size—that's okay).

4. **Mix the filling.** Toward the end of the rise time, in a small bowl, whisk together the melted butter, both sugars, flour, and cinnamon until no lumps remain and a thick paste forms. (If the filling is very soupy, pop it in the fridge for 3 to 5 minutes and whisk it again before using. If the filling is too firm, microwave for 10 seconds to loosen it into a paste.)

recipe continues

FILLING

28g (2 tablespoons) unsalted butter, *melted*

18g (1½ tablespoons packed) brown sugar

18g (1½ tablespoons) granulated sugar

7g (scant 1 tablespoon) all-purpose flour

6g (2 teaspoons) ground cinnamon

TOPPING

30g (2 tablespoons) whole milk

ICING

28g (2 tablespoons) brick-style cream cheese

60g (scant ½ cup) powdered sugar, *sifted*

5g (1 teaspoon) whole milk

¼ teaspoon vanilla extract

5. Shape. Grease a 5- or 6-inch square baking dish with cooking spray. Follow the instructions in photos 1 through 4 for shaping and cutting the cinnamon rolls.

6. Second rise. Loosely cover the baking dish and place in a warm spot to rise until the cinnamon rolls just about double in size, 1½ to 2 hours.

7. Preheat. Toward the end of the rise time, preheat the oven to 375°F.

8. Top and bake. Immediately before baking, drizzle the milk over the cinnamon rolls. Bake until the rolls are golden brown on top, 20 to 22 minutes. Set the baking dish on a wire rack to cool just slightly—about 15 minutes—before icing.

9. Ice the rolls. In a microwave-safe medium bowl, microwave the cream cheese for 5 to 10 seconds, just until it's softened. Whisk in the sifted powdered sugar, milk, and vanilla until a thick icing forms. Spread the icing all over the cinnamon rolls while they're still warm. Let cool for another 15 minutes or so before serving. Cinnamon rolls are best enjoyed warm!

1

On a lightly floured counter, press and roll the dough into a 13 by 7-inch rectangle with one of the short sides closest to you. Spread the surface of the dough with a thin layer of the filling all the way to three of the edges, leaving a ¼-inch strip of dough bare along the opposite short edge. Brush that bare strip of dough lightly with water.

2

Starting with the short edge of dough that's covered with filling, roll the dough into a tight log, using your hands as guards along the edges to keep them even as you roll. Roll the log onto the strip of dampened, bare dough to seal the seam underneath.

3

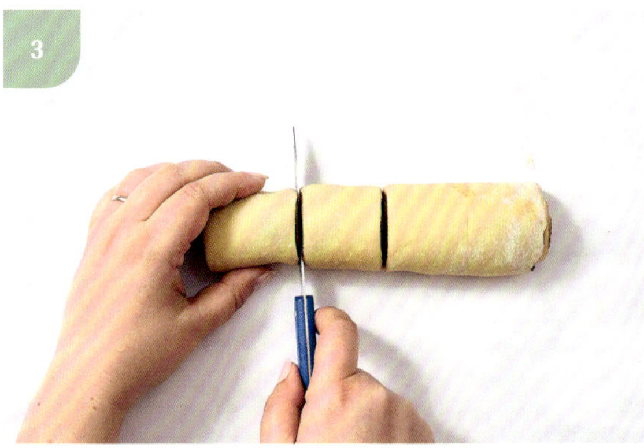

Use a sharp knife in a sawing motion to cut the log of dough into 4 segments, each about 2 inches wide. (Alternatively, you can use unwaxed, unflavored dental floss, looped around the log and pulled tight, to cut the rolls.)

4

Place the rolls spiral side up in the greased baking dish, pressing down gently on the top of each one.

CINNAMON SWIRL BREAD

MAKES
1 SMALL LOAF

RISING TIME:
2½ TO 3 HOURS

BAKE TIME:
20 TO 22 MINUTES

DOUGH

180g (1½ cups)
all-purpose flour
+ more for dusting

8g (2 teaspoons) sugar

3g (1 teaspoon)
instant yeast

3g (1 teaspoon)
Diamond Crystal
kosher salt

3g (1 teaspoon)
ground cinnamon

110g (⅓ cup
+ 2 tablespoons)
warm water (90°F)

8g (2 teaspoons)
olive oil

Cooking spray

FILLING

36g (3 tablespoons)
sugar

6g (2 teaspoons)
ground cinnamon

7g (scant 1 tablespoon)
all-purpose flour

Water (for spritzing)

To maximize the ratio of cinnamon-sugar swirl to cinnamon bread, this adorable cinnamon swirl loaf has two layers of cinnamon-sugar mixture spiraled inside. The filling turns to liquid in the oven, so poking holes through the top before baking allows steam to escape while it bakes, preventing pesky gaps from appearing in the swirl. Adding a bit of flour to the cinnamon-sugar filling and spritzing it with water during shaping makes the flour act like a glue between the dough layers, which also helps prevent annoying gaps. Science!

Get creative by subbing in your favorite apple pie spice, pumpkin pie spice, or even speculaas spice blend for the cinnamon!

1. **Make the dough.** Follow the instructions in Four-Inch Sandwich Bread (page 58) through step 3 (First Rise), adding the cinnamon to the dry ingredients in step 1 (Mix the Dough).

2. **Make the filling.** Toward the end of the rise time, in a small bowl, whisk together the sugar, cinnamon, and flour. Set aside.

3. **Shape.** Fill a spray bottle with water (if you don't have one, you can use a small bowl of water and a pastry brush). Turn the dough out onto a clean surface. Press and roll it into a 13 by 7-inch rectangle with one of the short sides closest to you. Follow the instructions in photos 1 through 3 to fill and shape the cinnamon swirl loaf.

4. **Second rise.** Grease a 4-inch square Pullman loaf pan with cooking spray. Place the loaf seam-side down in the prepared pan. Cover and let rise in a warm spot until the top of the loaf is about 1 inch below the rim of the pan, 1½ to 2 hours. (If your pan has a hole in the bottom, place it on a sheet pan to catch any leaks when baking.)

5. **Preheat.** Toward the end of the rise time, preheat the oven to 375°F.

6. **Bake.** Immediately before baking, use a toothpick or skewer to poke 3 holes as deep as you can into the loaf (photo 4). Spritz or brush the top of the loaf with water, then sprinkle any remaining cinnamon-sugar filling on top. Bake until golden brown on top, 20 to 22 minutes. Remove from the oven and let the loaf cool in the pan on a wire rack for 10 minutes, then turn it out onto the rack and let cool completely before slicing.

Spritz or brush the entire surface of the dough with water, then sprinkle about 2 tablespoons of the filling in a 3-inch-wide column down the center of the dough. Spritz the top of the filling well with water.

Fold the two bare edges of the dough over the filling and pinch the edges together. Spritz or brush the surface of the dough with water, sprinkle with another 2 tablespoons of the filling, this time all the way to the edges.

Spritz the top of the cinnamon-sugar mixture well with water, then carefully roll up into a log. Try not to put too much tension on the dough as you roll, and keep your hands on either side of it to guide it into an even log.

Poke 3 holes down the center of the bread, as deep as you can. This allows steam to escape and reduces the chance of gapping between the layers.

FOUR-STRAND
ROUND CHALLAH

CINNAMON
SWIRL BREAD

FOUR~STRAND ROUND CHALLAH

MAKES
1 SMALL LOAF

RISING TIME:
2 TO 4 HOURS

BAKE TIME:
17 TO 20 MINUTES

While lots of breads are braided, the hallmark of a challah dough is its lack of dairy products. Challah is enriched with egg, olive oil, and honey—no milk or butter in sight. As the traditional bread of weekly Jewish Shabbat dinners, it's important that challah be dairy-free so that it can be eaten with meat products (part of keeping kosher is not mixing meat and milk).

This mini challah is perfect for tearing and sharing at a small Shabbat dinner, but it's also great for making grilled cheese sandwiches and French toast!

120g (1 cup) bread flour + more for dusting

3g (1 teaspoon) instant yeast

3g (1 teaspoon) Diamond Crystal kosher salt

50g (3 tablespoons + 2 teaspoons; see Note) warm water (90°F)

10g (2¼ teaspoons) olive oil

6g (scant 1 teaspoon) honey

1 large egg yolk, *at room temperature*

Cooking spray

Egg wash: 1 large egg white, *beaten well*

1. **Mix.** In a medium bowl, whisk together the dry ingredients. Make a well in the center and add the warm water, olive oil, honey, and egg yolk. Use a dough whisk or a fork to mix until the mixture is crumbly, then use a bowl scraper or your hand to fold the dough over itself until patchy and dry but combined. It's okay if there's some loose flour in the bowl.

2. **Knead.** Turn the dough onto a lightly floured surface and knead until smooth and slightly tacky to the touch, 2 to 3 minutes. Lightly dust with more flour only as needed to prevent sticking.

3. **First rise.** Shape the dough into a ball and return to the bowl, cover, and let rise in a warm spot until it passes the Fingerprint Test (page 20), 1 to 2 hours (it may not truly double in size).

4. **Preshape.** Divide the dough into 4 equal portions using a bench scraper (each piece should weigh about 52 grams). On an unfloured clean surface, gently flatten each piece into a long rectangular shape. Starting with a long side, roll the dough into a log, pressing with your fingertips each time you roll it forward to seal the log shut.

5. **Shape.** Roll each log into a tapered rope about 10 inches long (try to keep the "seam" of the dough against the counter so it seals shut). If the ropes resist being rolled long enough, cover them loosely with a damp paper towel and let them rest for 1 to 2 minutes, then resume rolling. Follow the instructions in photos 1 through 4 to shape a round braided loaf.

6. **Second rise.** Line a baking sheet with parchment paper. Place the challah on the prepared pan, spray the top lightly with cooking spray, cover it loosely with plastic wrap, and let it rise until it's doubled in size and looks quite puffy, 1 to 2 hours.

7. **Preheat.** During the final 30 minutes of rise time, preheat the oven to 350°F.

8. **Bake.** Lightly brush the egg wash all over the challah. Bake until golden brown and shiny on top, 17 to 20 minutes. Transfer to a wire rack and let cool completely.

Recipe Notes

- Eagle-eyed readers will note that according to the conversion chart on page 27 50g water should technically be 3 tablespoons + 1 teaspoon by volume. In my testing I found that, if you're making this recipe using volume measurements, the extra-thirsty bread flour really does need an extra teaspoon of water.
- Challah, like other enriched doughs, is super versatile when it comes to shaping—you can get creative with braids, twists, loaves, buns, etc.

Arrange the 4 strands in a "#" shape, weaving them under and over each other. The center "window" of the "#" should be about 1-inch square.

Take the "under" strand from each pair and cross it over its neighbor, moving in the same direction with each crossed rope.

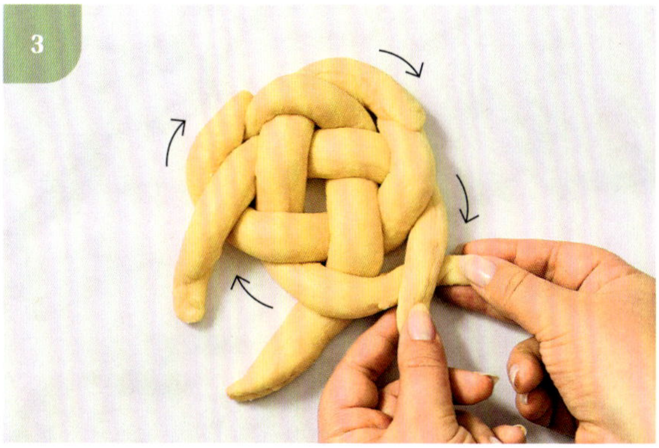

Take the new "under" strands and cross them over their neighbors, this time moving in the opposite direction around the circle.

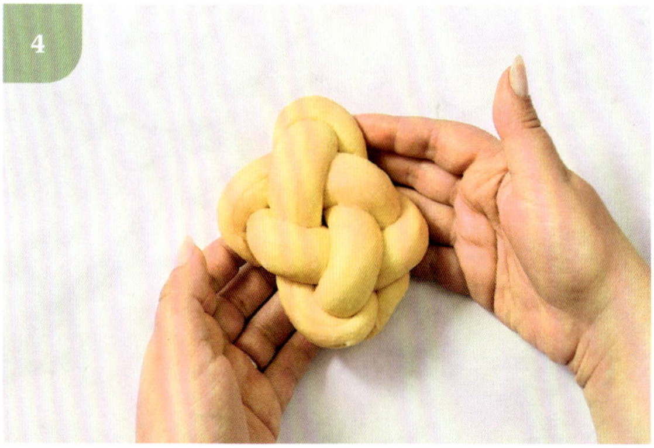

Pinch the remaining crossed pair of ropes together, stretching them gently to meet each other if needed, then tuck the joined ends under the loaf.

MINI CHOCOLATE BABKA

MAKES
1 SMALL LOAF

RISING TIME:
3 HOURS

BAKE TIME:
28 TO 30 MINUTES

DOUGH

Classic Brioche Dough (page 65)

Cooking spray

Egg wash: 1 large egg, *beaten well*

FILLING

28g (2 tablespoons) unsalted butter

65g (⅓ cup) semisweet chocolate chips

3g (1 teaspoon) ground cinnamon

¼ teaspoon vanilla extract

Pinch of salt

SYRUP

36g (3 tablespoons) sugar

35g (2 tablespoons + 1 teaspoon) water

¼ teaspoon vanilla extract

When I set out to make a list of recipes for this book, babka was one of the first I added to my list. If you've never had it before, it's a sweet, braided bread made using an enriched dough (in this case, brioche) and often filled with chocolate, nuts, jams, and fruits, though savory babkas exist, too.

You'd think after all this time I'd stop being surprised at just how substantial a loaf one cup of flour can produce, but this mini babka shocked and delighted even me with just how satisfyingly *big* it turned out given its scaled-back nature. You'd never guess it was made with just a cup of flour. I kept the filling simple, but you can absolutely top the chocolate filling with orange zest, nuts, shredded coconut, sesame seeds, sprinkles, chopped cookies, or anything else your heart desires.

1. **Make the dough.** Follow the instructions in Classic Brioche Loaf (page 65) through step 5 (First Rise).

2. **Make the filling.** Toward the end of the rise time, in a microwave-safe medium bowl, melt the butter. Add the chocolate chips, cinnamon, vanilla, and salt. Cover and let rest for 5 minutes, then stir slowly until the chocolate melts into a glossy sauce. (If needed, microwave for another 5 to 10 seconds and then stir again to help the chocolate melt.) Set aside.

3. **Preshape and fill.** On a lightly floured surface, roll the dough into a 10-inch square, tugging lightly at the corners to create sharp corners (the dough will be very thin). Preshape and fill the dough following the instructions in photo 1.

4. **Chill.** Lift the log of dough onto a sheet pan and place it in the fridge, uncovered, for 10 minutes to firm up before shaping.

5. **Shape.** Shape the babka into a coiled twist following the instructions in photos 2 through 4.

6. **Second rise.** Lightly spray a 4-inch square Pullman loaf pan with cooking spray, then place the coiled babka inside. Cover and let rise until the dough reaches 1 to 1½ inches below the rim of the pan, 1½ to 2 hours. If it's cold in your kitchen, the dough may not rise a lot, but that's okay.

recipe continues

7. **Preheat.** Toward the end of the rise time, preheat the oven to 350°F.

8. **Make the syrup.** While the oven heats, in a small microwave-safe bowl, stir together the sugar, water, and vanilla. Microwave in 20-second bursts, stirring well in between, until the sugar is completely dissolved. Set the syrup aside to cool and thicken for at least 20 minutes before use.

9. **Bake.** Immediately before baking, brush the surface of the babka with the egg wash. If your baking pan has a hole in the bottom, place it on a sheet pan to contain any leakage. Bake until deeply browned on top, 28 to 30 minutes. When the babka comes out of the oven, immediately brush the top with the sugar syrup, then drizzle the remaining syrup all over the loaf. Let the babka cool in the pan for 15 minutes, then use a knife or spatula to gently loosen it from the sides of the pan and turn it out onto a wire rack. Let cool completely before serving.

Recipe Note

If you don't have the square Pullman pan, you can stop the shaping step once the split halves of the dough are twisted together (photo 3) and place the babka in an 8 by 4-inch loaf pan. Then follow the rest of the recipe as written. It won't fill out the whole pan, but it makes a more substantial loaf than you'd think!

Use a mini offset spatula or table knife to spread the filling over the surface of the dough, all the way to three of the edges, leaving a ¼-inch strip bare along one edge. Gently roll up the dough, ending by rolling onto the bare strip of dough.

Use a bench scraper or a sharp knife to divide the chilled log of dough in half lengthwise. Turn the two halves so the insides are facing up.

Pinch the top ends of the two ropes together (it's okay if they don't totally stick to each other). Cross the ropes over each other to make a tight twist, again keeping the insides facing up. Repeat two more times, to get at least three twists down the length of the strips.

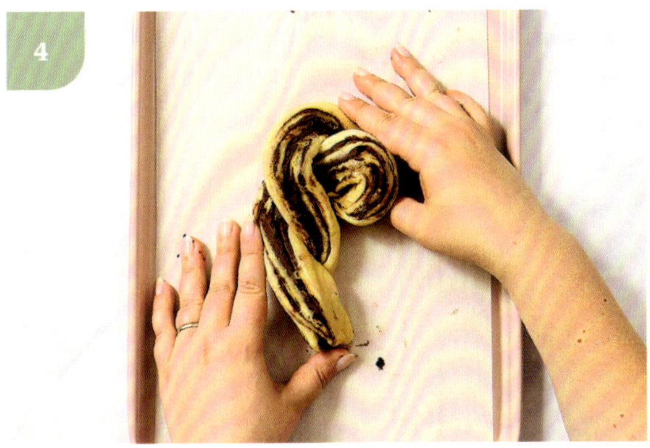

Take one end of the twisted rope and coil it into itself, always keeping the insides facing up, until you have a tightly coiled round of dough. Tuck the tail end of the rope underneath the coil slightly to hold it in place.

CHAPTER 4

FLATBREADS, CRACKERS, AND PIZZA

NO-KNEAD NAAN

MAKES
2 NAAN

RISING TIME:
2 TO 2½ HOURS

BAKE TIME:
3 TO 4 MINUTES

Naan gets its signature tenderness and buttery flavor from ghee (clarified butter) and whole-milk yogurt in the dough. While it's traditionally cooked in the high heat of a clay tandoor oven, this recipe cooks the naan under the broiler on a preheated baking steel. (If you don't have a baking steel, you can also use a baking stone or even an inverted sheet pan if that's all you've got.) Buttery and bubbly, this homemade naan is excellent for scooping up curries and dipping in raita.

DOUGH

120g (1 cup)
all-purpose flour
+ more for dusting

3g (1 teaspoon)
Diamond Crystal
kosher salt

3g (1 teaspoon)
instant yeast

2g (½ teaspoon)
sugar

85g (⅓ cup
+ 1 teaspoon)
warm water (90°F)

20g (1 heaping
tablespoon)
whole-milk
Greek yogurt

10g (2 teaspoons)
ghee or clarified
butter, *melted*
+ more for your hands

TOPPING

10g (2 teaspoons)
ghee, *melted*

Optional: Flaky salt,
garlic salt or minced
garlic, chopped fresh
herbs, cheese, etc.

1. Mix. In a medium bowl, whisk together the dry ingredients. Make a well in the center and add the warm water, yogurt, and melted ghee. Use a dough whisk or a fork to stir the liquid in the center, slowly incorporating flour from the sides of the bowl until a wet, sticky dough forms.

2. First rise. Gather the messy dough together at the bottom of the bowl. Cover and let rise at room temperature until almost doubled in size, 1 to 1½ hours. (It's a bit hard to tell when the dough is truly doubled, but as long as it's grown a bit and had time to rest, it'll be fine.)

3. Preshape. Scrape the sticky dough out onto a well-floured work surface. Divide it in half using a bench scraper (each piece should weigh about 121 grams). Follow the instructions in photo 1 to shape each piece into a loose ball.

4. Second rise. Invert the bowl over the 2 dough balls and let them rest for 30 minutes.

5. Preheat. As soon as you cover the dough balls, preheat the oven to 500°F with a baking steel on a rack about 7 inches below your oven's broiler. *Make sure the baking steel has at least 30 minutes to preheat once the oven is at temperature.*

6. Shape. Line a pizza peel or a flipped-over sheet pan with parchment paper. Grease your hands with a little bit of melted ghee and gently deflate each dough ball with your fingertips. Shape the naan following the instructions in photos 2 and 3. These don't have to look perfect, but try not to stretch the dough too thin in any spots. If the dough tears, just pinch it back together.

recipe continues

7. Third rise. Place the two stretched pieces of naan on the prepared pizza peel. Cover them lightly with a clean kitchen towel and let rest for another 30 minutes at room temperature.

8. Bake. Turn your oven's broiler on high for 1 minute. Slide the parchment paper off the pizza peel and directly onto the preheated baking steel. Broil until puffed up on top and spotty brown on the bottom, about 2 minutes, then use a pair of tongs to flip and broil for 1 to 2 minutes more. Check on the naan every 20 to 30 seconds after you flip it—broilers are HOT and things can go from golden brown to charred quickly!

9. Finish. Use the tongs to tug the parchment paper off the baking steel and back onto the pizza peel to remove the naan from the oven. Brush immediately with additional melted ghee and sprinkle with any other toppings you like. Let cool slightly before serving.

Recipe Note

Most parchment paper is safe up to 425° to 450°F. In this recipe it's under the broiler for such a short time that it won't burst into flames, but it will be quite browned when you pull it out. That's normal. If you're concerned, omit the parchment paper and just know your naan might brown faster than the recipe says.

Use floured hands to fold the edges of each piece of dough together in the center, pinching to form loose dough balls. Flip the balls over so the pinched seams are against the counter. Dust the tops lightly with flour. Handle the dough lightly and as little as possible so you don't press too much air out!

Press and stretch the dough flat, gripping lightly between the heels of your hands and flat fingertips.

Use a gentle grip to flatten, tug, and stretch the dough into a loose teardrop or oval shape about 10 inches long and 5 inches wide.

SKILLET FLATBREADS

MAKES
4 SMALL FLATBREADS

RISING TIME:
40 MINUTES

COOK TIME:
12 MINUTES TOTAL

These adorable little flatbreads can be on your table in less than an hour! They are fantastic for dipping in seasoned oil, scooping up heaps of hummus, or for topping with a swirl of Greek yogurt or cottage cheese and a drizzle of olive oil for a snack.

Instead of yeast, a bit of baking powder is all you need for leavening. For more buttery naan-like flatbreads, you can use melted clarified butter or ghee in place of oil, or if you've got any infused oils in your kitchen, this is a great time to break them out—garlic oil, chili oil, sun-dried tomato oil, and herb oils are all great ways to flavor your flatbreads!

120g (1 cup)
all-purpose flour
+ more for dusting

3g (1 teaspoon)
Diamond Crystal
kosher salt

6g (1½ teaspoons)
baking powder

75g (¼ cup
+ 1 tablespoon)
cool water (70°F)

12g (1 tablespoon)
olive oil + more for
your hands, the pan,
and brushing on top

Toppings: Za'atar, sesame seeds, everything bagel seasoning, rosemary, Parmesan cheese, garlic powder, dried minced onion, dried minced garlic, flaky salt, fresh herbs, herbes de Provence, berbere, etc.

1. **Mix.** In a medium bowl, whisk together the dry ingredients. Make a well in the center and add the water and olive oil. Use a dough whisk or a fork to mix until large clumps form and the water is fully absorbed. Then use a bowl scraper or your hand to fold the dough over itself in the bowl until it is mostly combined with a few dry bits remaining.

2. **Knead.** Turn the dough out onto a clean surface and knead until it becomes very smooth and soft to the touch, 3 to 4 minutes. Lightly dust more flour onto the counter only as needed to prevent sticking.

3. **First rest.** Shape the dough into a ball, dust it lightly with flour, and invert the bowl over it. Let the dough rest for 10 minutes.

4. **Preshape.** Divide the dough into 4 equal pieces using a bench scraper (each piece should weigh about 55 grams). Shape each piece into a tight ball (see page 34) with a barely visible seam underneath. Rub your hands with a few drops of oil and roll each dough ball around in your palms to coat in a light film of oil.

5. **Second rest.** Invert the bowl over the 4 dough balls and let them rest for 10 minutes.

6. **Shape.** Roll each dough ball into a 4-inch round, rotating the dough a quarter-turn between the rolls and always rolling from the center outward. Follow the instructions in photo 1 to stretch the flatbreads into ovals. Don't worry about them looking perfect—these are meant to be rustic!

recipe continues

7. Third rest. Cover the 4 stretched pieces of dough with damp paper towels and let them rest for 10 minutes.

8. Preheat. About halfway through the final 10 minutes of resting time, preheat a griddle or 10-inch cast-iron skillet over medium-low heat until water droplets flicked onto the surface sizzle and evaporate immediately on contact.

9. Cook. Brush the top side of each stretched piece of dough with olive oil and sprinkle with any toppings you like. Then brush the surface of the skillet with a thin layer of oil. Stretch each piece of dough gently as you place it in the skillet, seasoning-side up. (You can usually fit two flatbreads in a 10-inch skillet, so you'll need to cook the flatbreads in two batches if using one.) Cook until the bottoms are a spotty golden brown (photo 2), 2½ to 3 minutes. (Stoves can vary, so adjust your heat as needed to prevent burning!) Flip the flatbreads, brush the tops with more oil, and cook until the second side is spotty golden brown, 1½ to 3 minutes.

10. Steam. Transfer the finished flatbreads to a clean, dry kitchen towel and wrap them loosely to steam for at least 10 minutes before serving (this keeps them nice and flexible!).

Use your hands to lift and stretch each dough round into a roughly 3 by 5-inch oval, similar to how you'd stretch Silly Putty as a kid, curling your fingers around the edges and gradually spreading your knuckles apart to create a *slightly* thinner center. The dough will shrink back as it rests.

Cook the flatbreads until both sides are a spotty golden brown. If the flatbreads seem like they're getting too dark too quickly, adjust the heat to prevent them from burning.

A DEMURE LEAF OF FOUGASSE

MAKES
1 SMALL LOAF

RISING TIME:
1½ HOURS

BAKE TIME:
11 TO 14 MINUTES

Fougasse is a French flatbread cut into the shape of a leaf and baked until quite crusty. You can get creative with the leaf-shape designs, but I kept this one relatively simple to start you off. Fougasse is a great appetizer bread, perfect for tearing apart and dipping in oil or served alongside a charcuterie board (or in the case of this small-batch version, a very filling "girl dinner"). Herbes de Provence is a traditional seasoning for fougasse, but you can also get creative and add grated cheese, olives, capers, chopped nuts, lemon zest, or other spice and seasoning blends if you like.

DOUGH

120g (1 cup)
all-purpose flour
+ more for dusting

4g (1 teaspoon
+ heaping ¼ teaspoon)
Diamond Crystal
kosher salt

3g (1 teaspoon)
instant yeast

2g (2 teaspoons) herbes
de Provence

95g (⅓ cup
+ 1 tablespoon)
warm water (90°F)

4g (1 teaspoon)
olive oil

TOPPING

4g (1 teaspoon)
olive oil

½ teaspoon
herbes de Provence

Pinch of flaky
sea salt

1. **Mix.** In a medium bowl, whisk together the flour, kosher salt, yeast, and herbes de Provence. Make a well in the center and pour in the warm water and olive oil. Use a dough whisk or a fork to stir the liquid in the center, slowly incorporating flour from the sides of the bowl until a sticky dough forms. Gather the dough in a messy ball at the bottom of the bowl. Cover the bowl and let the dough rest for 20 minutes.

2. **First set of folds.** Use a damp hand to perform a series of stretch and folds (see page 31) in the bowl. Finish by flipping the dough over so the seam is underneath. Cover the bowl and let the dough rest for 20 minutes.

3. **Second set of folds.** Use a damp hand to perform a series of slap and folds (see page 30) in the bowl, again finishing with the seam tucked underneath the dough. The dough will still be sticky, but should feel smoother and stronger. Cover the bowl and let the dough rest for 20 minutes.

4. **Preheat.** Preheat the oven to 500°F with a baking steel, baking stone, or inverted sheet pan on the middle oven rack. Line a sheet pan with parchment paper.

5. **Shape.** Dust the top of the dough in the bowl generously with flour, then tip it out onto the prepared pan. Dust the now-sticky top side of the dough generously with flour, too, then follow the instructions in photo 1 to create the leaf shape. Follow the instructions in photos 2 through 4 to cut the leaf pattern into the stretched dough. The dough is sticky and can sometimes cling to the knife. Dust in more flour if needed to help keep the dough from sticking to itself, and be patient with yourself and the dough!

6. **Rest.** Cover the dough loosely with plastic wrap or a clean kitchen towel and let rest for 30 minutes.

recipe continues

7. Bake. Brush the dough lightly with 4 grams of olive oil and sprinkle with ½ teaspoon herbes de Provence and a pinch of flaky sea salt. Slide the sheet pan directly onto the preheated baking steel and bake until the fougasse is golden brown and puffed up, 11 to 14 minutes. Let it cool on the sheet pan for at least 10 minutes before serving.

Use damp hands to gently prod and stretch the dough into a triangular leaf-like shape that's about 8 to 9 inches from tip to base and 6 to 7 inches across at its widest.

Use a bench scraper or a sharp knife to cut down the middle of the leaf shape, leaving the two ends intact, wiggling the blade side to side to nudge the dough apart to open a long hole in the center.

Then use a smaller knife or the edge of a small metal spatula to cut and wiggle apart three angled cuts on either side of the center slash to make the "veins" of the leaf.

Use flour-dusted fingers as needed to help stretch the holes apart.

FLUFFY PITA POCKETS

MAKES
2 PITA POCKETS

RISING TIME:
1 HOUR 45 MINUTES TO
2 HOURS 50 MINUTES

BAKE TIME:
5 TO 7 MINUTES

Though pita has been made in the Mediterranean and Middle East for millennia, half the fun of making pita from scratch today is getting to watch it balloon up through the glass door of your modern oven. Whether you tear this pita into pieces to dip it in hummus or stuff it full of your favorite sandwich fillings, you'll love just how soft and fluffy the insides are. A small amount of whole wheat flour adds a ton of flavor, but if you don't have it on hand, you can replace it with all-purpose flour.

My best pro tip for making stuffed pita pocket sandwiches: Trim off just the top inch of the pita pocket and use it to line the inside—this reinforces the bottom seam to prevent blowouts. You're welcome!

100g (¾ cup + 4 teaspoons) all-purpose flour + more for dusting

20g (2 tablespoons + 2 teaspoons) whole wheat flour

5g (1¼ teaspoons) sugar

4g (1 teaspoon + heaping ¼ teaspoon) Diamond Crystal kosher salt

2g (heaping ½ teaspoon) instant yeast

75g (¼ cup + 1 tablespoon) warm water (90°F)

8g (2 teaspoons) olive oil

Cooking spray

1. **Mix.** In a medium bowl, whisk together the dry ingredients. Make a well in the center and pour in the warm water and olive oil. Use a dough whisk or a fork to stir the liquid in the center, slowly incorporating flour from the sides of the bowl until large clumps form. Switch to a bowl scraper or your hand and repeatedly fold the dough over itself in the bowl until it comes together.

2. **Knead.** Turn the dough out onto a lightly floured surface. Knead until smooth and just slightly tacky to the touch, dusting in additional flour only as needed to prevent sticking. It's okay if the dough leaves a slight residue on your palms, but it shouldn't be sticking to the table or pulling away on your hands.

3. **First rise.** Shape the dough into a ball. Lightly grease the bowl with a thin film of cooking spray. Place the dough ball in the bowl, seam-side down. Cover the bowl and let the dough rise at room temperature until it doubles in size and the dough passes the Fingerprint Test (page 20), 1 to 1½ hours.

4. **Preheat.** Toward the end of the rise time, preheat the oven to 500°F with a baking steel, baking stone, or inverted sheet pan on the middle oven rack. Make sure the oven preheats at temperature for at least 30 minutes before baking your pita.

5. **Preshape.** Divide the dough in half using a bench scraper (each piece should weigh about 107 grams). Working on a clean, unfloured surface, shape each piece into a very tight ball (see page 34), making sure the seam underneath is pretty much invisible after you're done shaping. Place the dough balls seam-side down on the counter and dust the tops with flour. Invert the bowl over the dough balls and let them rest for 10 minutes. If the seam is still visible after 10 minutes, let them rest for an additional 5 to 10 minutes until it looks sealed shut.

6. **Shape.** Dust the dough balls with more flour. Roll each one from the center out, rotating a quarter-turn after each roll, until they're each about 4 inches wide—do not run the rolling pin off the edges of the dough! Once they're both 4 inches across, alternate between the pieces of dough, rolling each one about an inch wider and letting it rest while you roll the other, until both pieces are 6 to 7 inches in diameter. They may have a bit of a thicker edge around the rim, and that's okay.

7. **Second rise.** Transfer the pitas to a sheet pan, dust them lightly with flour, cover them loosely with plastic wrap, and let them rest until they're slightly puffy around the edges, about 20 minutes.

8. **Bake.** Remove the plastic wrap and slide the sheet pan directly onto the preheated baking steel. Bake the pitas until they balloon up and turn a pale golden color, 5 to 7 minutes. (They may not puff until the final minute or so!)

9. **Steam.** Remove the pitas from the oven and wrap them loosely in a clean kitchen towel to steam for at least 20 minutes before eating. (The steam helps them stay flexible and soft.)

FLOUR TORTILLAS

MAKES THREE 9-INCH TORTILLAS

RISING TIME: 30 MINUTES

COOK TIME: 8 MINUTES TOTAL

120g (1 cup) all-purpose flour + more for dusting

2g (heaping ½ teaspoon) Diamond Crystal kosher salt

2g (½ teaspoon) baking powder

70g (¼ cup + 2 teaspoons) cool water (70°F)

15g (1 tablespoon + ¾ teaspoon) shortening or lard, *melted* + more for your hands

When it came time to develop a flour tortilla recipe, I turned to prolific Latin American cookbook author Sandra Gutierrez, who recommended the Tortillas de Harina y Coco recipe from her cookbook *Latinisimo* as a starting point for a small-batch recipe. At her suggestion, I swapped out the coconut milk for water and the lard for shortening to make the recipe a bit more accessible (though you're welcome to use coconut milk and lard if you prefer). One note: No matter how thin you roll them, homemade tortillas tend to be a *bit* thicker than store-bought ones, but as long as you don't overcook them and don't skip the final steaming step they'll be just as soft and flexible!

1. **Mix.** In a medium bowl, whisk together the dry ingredients. Make a well in the center and pour in *half* (35g) of the cool water and *all* of the melted shortening. Use flat fingers to stir and smear the water and shortening into the dry ingredients until the water is absorbed (photo 1). Pour about half the remaining water (17g) onto the driest bits of flour in the bowl, mix again with your fingers, then add the rest of the water to any remaining dry bits and finish mixing with flat fingertips (photo 1) until the dough clumps together in a messy ball.

2. **Knead.** Turn the dough out onto a lightly floured surface, rub any excess dough off your fingers and onto the dough, and knead until the dough is very smooth, supple, and soft to the touch, 3 to 4 minutes. Lightly dust more flour onto the counter as needed to prevent sticking.

3. **First rest.** Knead the dough into a ball, dust it lightly with flour, and place it seam-side down on the counter. Invert the bowl over it and let the dough rest for 10 minutes.

4. **Preshape.** Divide the dough into 3 equal pieces using a bench scraper (each piece should weigh about 69 grams). Shape each piece into a tight ball (see page 34) with a barely visible seam underneath. Rub your hands with a small amount of shortening, then roll each dough ball around in your hands to coat them with a thin film of shortening.

5. **Second rest.** Invert the bowl over the 3 dough balls and let them rest for 20 minutes.

recipe continues

6. Preheat. Preheat a griddle or 10-inch cast-iron skillet over medium-low heat until water droplets flicked on the surface sizzle and evaporate immediately on contact. Lightly dampen a clean kitchen towel and lay it out nearby—you'll use it to wrap the finished tortillas to steam when they're done cooking.

7. Shape. While the pan heats, generously flour a clean countertop and roll each dough ball into about a 5-inch round (photo 2). Pick which tortilla you're going to cook first and roll it into a 9-inch round, always rolling from the center out and rotating the dough a quarter-turn after each roll to maintain a round shape. Do not roll off the edges of the dough. The dough will shrink back as you roll; if it shrinks back too much, move on to the next one and let this one rest for a bit before you resume rolling.

8. Cook. Carefully slide the first tortilla onto your palm with your fingers spread wide to support it. Flip or slide it off your hand and into the pan, carefully adjusting the edges if needed so it lies flat. Cook until you see pale golden flecks on the bottom and bubbles on the top, about 1 minute (photo 3). Use a fish spatula to flip the tortilla and cook until you see pale golden flecks on the bottom (some of the bubbles will inflate more as the tortilla cooks), about 1 minute. Flip one more time and cook for another 10 seconds.

9. Steam. Transfer the finished tortilla to the damp kitchen towel and wrap loosely. Repeat with the remaining two pieces of dough, adjusting the heat as needed to prevent burning. Let the tortillas steam for at least 20 minutes before eating to keep them soft and flexible!

Recipe Note

For an even number of tortillas, you can divide the dough into 4 pieces (51 grams each) instead. The cook time may be slightly shorter, but you'll still want to roll them as thin as possible, about 8 inches across instead of 9 inches.

Use your flat fingers to stir and smear the water and shortening into the flour mixture.

Rotating the dough a quarter-turn after each roll prevents the dough from sticking to the counter and makes it easy to roll a nice even round.

The tortilla will get very bubbly as it cooks. Those bubbles help make the tortilla flexible even after it cools!

SINGLE SCALLION PANCAKE

MAKES ONE 9-INCH SCALLION PANCAKE

RESTING TIME: 31 MINUTES

COOK TIME: 4 TO 6 MINUTES

DOUGH

120g (1 cup) all-purpose flour + more for dusting

2g (heaping ½ teaspoon) Diamond Crystal kosher salt + more for finishing

88g (⅓ cup + 1½ teaspoons) boiling water (212°F)

1 to 2 tablespoons canola or vegetable oil (for the pan) + a few drops for your hands

Made with a beautifully supple hot-water dough, pan-fried scallion pancakes are one of my all-time favorite appetizers and street foods. The outside is crisp and flaky, while the center retains just a bit of satisfying chew, and they are *so good* dipped in a bit of seasoned soy sauce. The use of boiling water in the dough gelatinizes the starches in the flour, making a soft and pliable dough that holds its shape well.

To make the flaky layers, the dough is rolled whisper-thin and spread with a sesame oil paste, then sprinkled generously with thinly sliced scallions and rolled up before being coiled and rolled out again. For a bit of extra texture, sprinkle one side of the coiled dough with sesame seeds before rolling it into a round; they toast up beautifully in the pan!

1. **Mix.** In a medium bowl, whisk together the flour and salt. Make a well in the center and pour in the boiling water all at once. Use a dough whisk or a fork to mix the dough until medium-size clumps form and most of the dry flour is incorporated. Switch to a bowl scraper or your hand and fold the dough over itself in the bowl until it mostly comes together.

2. **Knead.** Turn the dough out onto a clean surface and knead until the dough smooths out, about 1 minute. Lightly dust more flour onto the counter only as needed to prevent sticking.

3. **First rest.** Tuck the dough into a ball, invert the bowl over it, and let it rest for 1 minute.

4. **Knead again.** Knead the dough for another 15 to 20 seconds—it should feel much smoother and more supple. Shape the dough into a ball with the seam tucked underneath.

5. **Second rest.** Drizzle your palms with a few drops of oil and roll the dough ball around in your hands to coat it with a thin film of oil. Place it back in the bowl, cover, and let it rest for 20 minutes at room temperature (it won't rise, but the starches will relax and hydrate as the dough rests).

recipe continues

FILLING

15g (1 tablespoon + ½ teaspoon) toasted sesame oil

5g (2 teaspoons) all-purpose flour

1g (heaping ¼ teaspoon) Diamond Crystal kosher salt

40g (scant ½ cup) thinly sliced scallion greens (from 5 to 6 scallions)

1 teaspoon sesame seeds (optional)

6. Mix the filling. While the dough rests, in a small bowl, stir together the toasted sesame oil, flour, and salt until combined. Set aside.

7. Preshape. Place the dough ball on a lightly floured work surface. Dust the top of the dough lightly with flour. Follow the shaping instructions in photos 1 through 4 to roll, fill, and coil the dough. Place the coiled dough on a floured surface, invert the bowl over it, and let it rest for 10 minutes.

8. Shape. Flour the top of the dough spiral and roll it into a 9-inch round, rotating the dough a quarter-turn after each roll. Dust lightly with additional flour only if needed to prevent sticking.

9. Preheat. Preheat a 10-inch skillet over medium-low heat until water droplets flicked on the surface sizzle and evaporate immediately on contact. Add the canola or vegetable oil, making sure you have a thin layer that covers the bottom of the pan. When the oil shimmers (or the tip of a wooden chopstick bubbles when placed in the oil), it's ready.

10. Cook. Line a plate with paper towels or set a wire rack in a sheet pan and have near the stove. Carefully place the scallion pancake in the skillet. Press down gently in the center with your fingertips or use a spatula to lift around the edges to make sure there aren't any air bubbles trapped underneath. Cook until deeply golden brown, 2 to 3 minutes per side (the parts in contact with the skillet will be dark golden brown, while other areas might be paler–that's okay). Rotate the pancake in the pan a few times as it cooks for even browning, and don't be afraid to take a peek underneath as it cooks so you can adjust the temperature or flip it sooner if it's browning too quickly. Transfer the scallion pancake to the paper towel or wire rack and sprinkle with a pinch of salt. Serve warm!

Roll the dough into a very thin rectangle about 16 by 9 inches. Don't worry if it's not perfect or if the dough wrinkles in a few places. Just focus on getting a nice even thinness across the dough. If the dough tears at all, pinch it back together.

Use a mini offset spatula or a pastry brush to gently spread the sesame oil mixture evenly over the surface of the dough. Sprinkle evenly with the sliced scallions and the sesame seeds (if using).

Starting on one of the long sides, roll the dough up into a tight rope. Once you have a good roll going, it helps to tug backward lightly before rolling forward to create an even tighter roll.

Coil the rope into a spiral shape, doing your best to keep the seam on the inside of the coil. Tuck the end of the rope under the spiraled dough, then place the spiral on a lightly floured counter.

ROSEMARY~OLIVE OIL CRACKERS

MAKES
28 CRACKERS

RESTING TIME:
30 MINUTES

BAKE TIME:
22 TO 27 MINUTES

120g (1 cup)
all-purpose flour
+ more for dusting

3g (1 teaspoon)
Diamond Crystal
kosher salt

2g (2 teaspoons)
dried or fresh rosemary,
leaves left whole
or minced

60g (¼ cup)
hot water (120°F)

12g (1 tablespoon)
olive oil + more for your
hands and for topping

½ teaspoon flaky
sea salt (for topping)

These crisp, slightly bubbly crackers are made from a simple olive oil dough with plenty of fragrant rosemary peeking through. My best advice to you: Take your time rolling out the dough; you need it to be *very thin* and getting there requires patience. I like to use a fluted pastry wheel to give the crackers a pretty zigzag edge, but a regular pizza wheel will work just fine, too.

Don't like rosemary? Fresh or dried thyme, tarragon, oregano, or basil (or a blend of herbs) are also great options here. Serve these with a bit of whipped goat cheese, your favorite charcuterie, and a drizzle of honey if you're feeling fancy.

1. **Preheat.** Preheat the oven to 350°F.

2. **Mix.** In a medium bowl, whisk together the flour, kosher salt, and rosemary. Make a well in the center and pour in the hot water and olive oil. Use a dough whisk or a fork to stir the liquid in the center, slowly incorporating flour from the sides of the bowl until a sticky dough forms. Switch to a bowl scraper or your hand and fold the dough over itself until it mostly comes together.

3. **Knead.** Turn the dough out onto a clean work surface and knead until it smooths out, 1 to 2 minutes. Resist adding more flour unless absolutely necessary. Finish by kneading the dough into a ball. Drizzle a few drops of olive oil onto your palms and roll the dough around in your hands to coat it with a thin film of oil.

4. **Rest.** Invert the bowl over the dough ball and let it rest on the counter for 30 minutes. The dough won't rise, but the gluten will relax and the starches will fully hydrate.

5. **Shape.** Lightly flour a sheet of parchment paper. Place the dough on the prepared parchment. Flour the top side of the dough lightly, then roll it into a rectangle about 14 by 10 inches (photo 1).

6. **Cut.** Cut the dough into crackers following the instructions in photo 2 (don't separate them!). Sprinkle the crackers evenly with the flaky sea salt.

7. **Bake.** Slide the sheet of parchment paper carefully onto a sheet pan. Bake until the crackers are pale golden brown around the edges and the ones in the center of the pan feel firm to the touch, 22 to 27 minutes. Let the crackers cool on the pan for 10 to 15 minutes, then use your hands to break them apart.

Kitchen Note

It's easier to cut the dough into crackers on the parchment paper before sliding the paper onto the sheet pan so that the rim of the sheet pan doesn't get in the way of your blade.

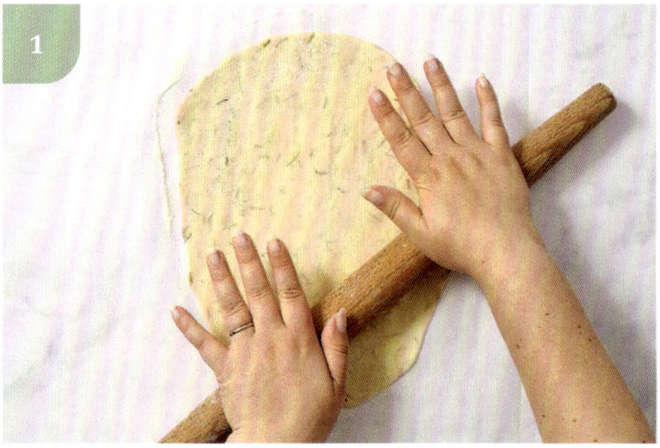

Roll the dough into a rectangle about 14 by 10 inches. It should be very, very thin—almost translucent. The dough will shrink back a bit as you roll, but if it feels like it's fighting you or is prone to tearing, let it rest for 30 to 60 seconds, then resume rolling.

Brush the surface of the dough lightly with olive oil, then use a fluted pastry wheel or a pizza cutter to cut the dough into rectangles about 3½ by 1½ inches. (Don't separate them yet!)

ROSEMARY–OLIVE
OIL CRACKERS

MATZOH FOR PASSOVER

MATZOH FOR PASSOVER

MAKES
4 MATZOH

RESTING TIME:
10 MINUTES

BAKE TIME:
12 TO 14 MINUTES TOTAL

120g (1 cup) all-purpose flour + more for dusting

Pinch of Diamond Crystal kosher salt

70g (¼ cup + 2 teaspoons) hot water (120°F)

2g (½ teaspoon) olive oil

Matzoh, the traditional unleavened "bread" of Passover, is the recipe I always point to as proof that even when bread goes "wrong," you can still style it into something edible. As the Passover story goes, when the Israelites fled enslavement by the pharaoh in Egypt, they didn't have time to let their bread rise and instead baked it off into flat, unleavened crackers known as matzoh. This recipe makes four pieces of matzoh, perfect for a very small seder—three for the center of the table, including a designated "middle" piece to break to make the *afikomen*, with one more left over for topping with *maror* (bitter herbs), *charoset* (chopped fruit and nuts), or, let's be honest, salted butter.

1. **Preheat.** Preheat a baking steel, baking stone, or inverted sheet pan in a 500°F oven for at least 30 minutes before mixing the dough.

2. **Mix.** In a medium bowl, whisk together the flour and salt. Make a well in the center and pour in the hot water and olive oil. Use a dough whisk or a fork to stir the liquid in the center, slowly incorporating flour from the sides of the bowl until a sticky dough forms. It's okay if there are still some loose bits of flour left.

3. **Knead.** Turn the dough out onto a clean surface and knead until it smooths out, 2 to 3 minutes. It will feel very wet and sticky at first, but will quickly become less sticky as the flour absorbs more of the water. Resist adding more flour unless absolutely necessary to prevent sticking.

4. **Preshape.** Use a bench scraper to divide the dough into 4 equal portions (each piece should weigh about 48 grams). Shape each piece into a tight ball (see page 34), pinching the seams together underneath.

5. **Rest.** Invert the bowl over the dough balls and let them rest on the counter for 10 to 20 minutes. The dough won't rise, but the gluten will relax and the starches will fully hydrate.

6. **Roll.** Generously flour your work surface. Roll out 1 matzoh following the instructions in photo 1.

7. Dock. Generously dock the matzoh following the instructions in photo 2. Carefully transfer the matzoh to a sheet of parchment paper.

8. Bake. Slide the parchment paper with the matzoh on it onto the preheated baking steel. Bake until the matzoh is golden brown around the edges and spotty across the surface, 3 to 3½ minutes (for a darker matzoh, feel free to cook longer). Transfer to a wire rack to cool, then repeat with the remaining dough balls, using a new sheet of parchment paper each time.

Kitchen Note

If rolling the dough on your work surface and transferring to parchment paper feels too tricky, you can roll it directly on the parchment paper instead.

Place 1 dough ball on the floured surface. Roll the dough from the center out, periodically lifting the dough and giving it a quarter-turn to prevent sticking and maintain an even thickness until you have a thin round of dough about 9 inches across.

Use a fork to generously dock (poke holes into) the entire surface of the dough. Then, however much docking you thought it needed, go back and dock it some more.

THIN~CRUST PIZZA

MAKES ONE
12- TO 14-INCH PIZZA

RISING TIME:
5½ HOURS+

BAKE TIME:
5 TO 8 MINUTES

AUTOLYSE

120g (1 cup) all-purpose flour (or replace half the all-purpose flour with type "00" pizza flour) + more for dusting

78g (scant ⅓ cup) warm water (90°F)

DOUGH

1g (heaping ¼ teaspoon) instant yeast

1g (¼ teaspoon) sugar

10g (2 teaspoons) warm water (90°F)

2g (heaping ½ teaspoon) Diamond Crystal kosher salt

2g (½ teaspoon) olive oil + more for the container

1½ teaspoons semolina flour or all-purpose flour (for the pizza peel)

To make a single batch of pizza dough that is super elastic, relaxed, and easy to stretch for a gorgeously thin New York–style crust, mixing the dough in two stages is crucial. By mixing the flour and water first, the starches in the dough have time to begin forming a gluten network before incorporating the yeast, sugar, oil, and salt, four ingredients that cause the dough to tighten up. The oil helps the dough develop a beautiful elasticity and the sugar helps the crust brown on the high heat (500°F+) of a preheated baking steel or baking stone, or in a home pizza oven. The long, cold rise in the fridge slows down the yeast activity, giving the dough more flavor and a more elastic texture. While you *can* use it after just four hours in the fridge, the longer you give it to rise in the fridge before stretching, the more relaxed and stretchy it will be!

1. **Autolyse.** Add the flour to a medium bowl. Add the warm water and use a dough whisk or a fork to mix until a stiff, dry dough forms. Smush it into a ball, cover the bowl, and let the dough rest for 10 minutes (this allows the flour to hydrate and the starches to begin aligning, making the dough easier to stretch later on).

2. **Proof yeast.** While the dough rests, mix the yeast, sugar, and 10g (2 teaspoons) of warm water in a separate small bowl. Cover and set aside until the autolyse is done. The yeast mixture will get very foamy and bubbly.

3. **Mix the dough.** Sprinkle the yeast mixture, salt, and olive oil over the dough. Use your thumb and forefinger like a pincer to pinch, squish, and fold the dough over itself in the bowl until the gritty salt texture disappears and the olive oil has been incorporated (photo 1). The dough will be wet and slippery. Shape it into a messy ball in the bottom of the bowl.

4. **First rest.** Cover the bowl and let the dough rest at room temperature for 10 minutes.

5. **Knead.** Turn the dough out onto a lightly floured surface and knead until smooth and slightly tacky to the touch, 2 to 3 minutes. Lightly dust more flour onto the counter only as needed to prevent sticking. You will feel the dough smooth out and soften pretty quickly as you work it.

recipe continues

SAUCE

61g (¼ cup) unsalted tomato sauce

1g (heaping ¼ teaspoon) Diamond Crystal kosher salt

⅛ teaspoon garlic powder

⅛ teaspoon dried oregano

⅛ teaspoon dried basil

TOPPINGS

113g (1 cup) low-moisture whole-milk mozzarella cheese, *shredded*

4g (1 heaping tablespoon) Parmesan or Pecorino Romano cheese, *finely grated*

Any other pizza toppings you like!

6. First rise. Shape the dough into a ball, place it back in the bowl with the seam side facing down, cover, and let rest somewhere warm until almost doubled in size, 1 to 1½ hours.

7. Preshape and second rest. Turn the dough out onto a lightly floured counter and shape it into a tight ball (see page 34). Lightly oil a 16-ounce deli container (or similar-size container with a lid). Place the dough inside the greased container, seam-side down, and let it rest in the fridge for at least 4 hours or up to 48 hours.

8. Second rise. Let the dough rest at room temperature for at least 45 minutes or up to 1 hour prior to stretching.

9. Preheat. An hour before you plan to make the pizza, begin preheating a baking steel or baking stone in a 500°F oven 7 to 9 inches below your oven's broiler unit (or on the lowest rack of your oven if you have a broiler drawer. If you have a broiler drawer, you'll also need to place an inverted sheet pan in there—you'll slide the pizza onto it for its final minute of cook time).

10. Make the sauce. In a small bowl, whisk together the tomato sauce, salt, garlic powder, oregano, and basil.

11. Stretch. Turn out the dough onto a very generously floured surface (about 2 tablespoons of flour). Generously flour the top and sides of the dough. Follow the instructions in photos 2 through 4 to stretch the dough. If at any point the dough feels fragile, set it down on the counter to rest for a few minutes. If it tears, place it down and pinch those spots back together, let it rest for 1 to 2 minutes, then resume stretching, taking extra care to be gentle on the pinched spots. When the dough is 12 to 14 inches across, sprinkle the pizza peel with the semolina flour and use your hand to spread it in an even layer. Transfer the stretched dough to the pizza peel.

12. Top. Dollop the pizza sauce over the surface of the crust, then use the back of a spoon to spread it in an even layer, leaving about ½ inch of crust bare around the edge. Top with the shredded mozzarella and finish with the Parmesan or Pecorino Romano.

13. Bake. Give the pizza a little shimmy on the peel to make sure it isn't stuck (if it is, carefully lift the stuck edge and dust additional flour underneath). Slide the pizza off the peel onto the baking steel. Cook for 2 to 3 minutes, then rotate the pizza on the baking steel and cook for 2 to 3 minutes more. Finish by broiling for 30 to 60 seconds, or until the cheese and crust are as browned on top as you like. Broilers are hot and can vary widely—check the pizza every 30 seconds once you begin broiling to make sure it doesn't burn!

Recipe Notes

- To freeze pizza dough, let it rise in the deli container for 1 hour at room temperature *before* placing in the freezer. To thaw, place the frozen dough in the fridge for a few hours or overnight.
- If your pizza dough is particularly active and eager to burst out of the container, gently deflate it, knead it back into a ball in the container, and return it to the fridge.
- If you don't have a pizza peel, an inverted sheet pan lined with parchment paper will work in a pinch.

Pinch and squish the dough, folding it over itself until the salt and olive oil are incorporated.

Use the pads of your fingers to gently press down in the center of the dough ball, rotating the dough on the counter as you work, leaving a 1-inch rim around the outside for the crust.

Gently lift the dough by one edge of the crust without smushing the thick outer rim, and let it hang down. Rotate it, using the pads of your fingers, letting gravity do the work for you.

Slide the dough onto the back of your hands with your fingers curved in (so you don't poke through the dough). Move your hands together, then apart, to stretch and rotate the dough.

CHAPTER 5

BISCUITS, PASTRIES, AND QUICK BREADS

CHEDDAR~CHIVE BUTTERMILK DROP BISCUITS

MAKES
5 BISCUITS

CHILL TIME:
20 MINUTES

BAKE TIME:
17 TO 19 MINUTES

DOUGH

120g (1 cup)
all-purpose flour

4g (1 teaspoon)
baking powder

3g (1 teaspoon)
Diamond Crystal
kosher salt

56g (4 tablespoons)
cold unsalted butter, ***cut into ¼-inch cubes***

42g (½ cup)
cold cheddar cheese, ***shredded***

4g (1½ tablespoons)
finely minced
fresh chives

113g (½ cup)
buttermilk, ***cold from the fridge***

TO FINISH

14g (1 tablespoon)
unsalted butter, ***melted***

Pinch of flaky sea salt (optional)

These just might be the easiest biscuits you'll ever make—there's absolutely no shaping required. Once you've stirred together the dough you drop it onto the sheet pan (hence DROP biscuits!) and bake. Consider this a base recipe to play around with a lot of other flavor combinations. For example, if you replace the chives with Old Bay, you'll end up with a dinner biscuit reminiscent of the ones you get at a restaurant whose name rhymes with Bed Mobster. Other great flavor combinations for these drop biscuits are bacon bits and Gruyère, dill and Havarti, and rosemary and Parmesan. Just as in any biscuit recipe, keep the butter and buttermilk as cold as possible and don't overwork the dough for the most tender results!

1. **Prep.** Line a sheet pan with parchment paper and set aside.

2. **Mix.** In a medium bowl, whisk together the flour, baking powder, and kosher salt. Add the cold cubed butter and use your fingers and thumbs to pinch and flatten the butter cubes, rubbing them into the flour until the biggest shards of butter are about the size of a dime (photo 1). Use a dough whisk or a fork to stir in the grated cheddar and minced chives. Make a well in the center and pour in the cold buttermilk. Mix the dough together just until combined. Do not overwork the dough—stop mixing once there are no visible dry bits and it has the texture of a thick paste (photo 2).

3. **Scoop.** Use a #20 (3-tablespoon) cookie scoop to portion 5 biscuits onto the prepared sheet pan. If you have any extra dough, divide it up among the biscuits.

4. **Chill.** Place the sheet pan, uncovered, in the freezer for 20 minutes.

5. **Preheat.** While the biscuits chill, preheat the oven to 425°F.

6. **Bake.** Bake the biscuits until lightly browned on top, 17 to 19 minutes. Immediately after they come out of the oven, spoon 1 tablespoon of melted butter over the biscuits and sprinkle with the flaky salt. Let the biscuits cool on the sheet pan for about 10 minutes before serving. Biscuits are best served warm!

Before adding the buttermilk, the butter and flour should look like coarse, clumpy sand with larger dime-size shards of butter throughout.

Stop mixing as soon as the dough resembles a thick, lumpy paste—if you overmix, your biscuits will end up tough!

FLAKY MINI BUTTERMILK BISCUITS
CHEDDAR-CHIVE BUTTERMILK DROP BISCUITS

FLAKY MINI BUTTERMILK BISCUITS

MAKES
4 ABOUT-2-INCH BISCUITS

CHILL TIME:
15 MINUTES

BAKE TIME:
16 TO 18 MINUTES

The tall, flaky layers in these miniature biscuits come from a technique I borrowed from the biscuit queen herself, my friend Cynthia Christensen of But First We Brunch! (ButFirstWeBrunch.com). Instead of more traditional letter folds for lamination, the biscuit dough is cut, stacked, and squished several times, creating flat layers of butter that turn to steam in the oven, pushing the dough apart into thin, flaky layers. Not only is this faster than a bunch of letter folds, it's a lot more fun! Serve these plush biscuits warm with gravy, topped with honey butter and jam, or alongside hot honey and fried chicken.

120g (1 cup)
all-purpose flour
+ more for dusting

4g (1 teaspoon)
granulated sugar

3g (1 teaspoon)
Diamond Crystal
kosher salt

3g (½ teaspoon
+ ⅛ teaspoon)
baking powder

56g (4 tablespoons)
cold unsalted butter,
cut into ¼-inch cubes

90g (⅓ cup + 1 scant
tablespoon) buttermilk,
cold from the fridge

Egg wash: 1 large egg,
beaten well

1 teaspoon
flaky sea salt
OR sparkling sugar
(for topping)

1. **Preheat.** Preheat the oven to 425°F. Line a sheet pan with parchment paper.

2. **Mix.** In a medium bowl, whisk together the flour, granulated sugar, kosher salt, and baking powder. Add the cold cubed butter and use your fingers to toss it in the flour to coat. Follow the instructions in photo 1 to smush in the butter. Make a well in the center and pour in the cold buttermilk. Use a dough whisk or a fork to mix just until the buttermilk is absorbed. The dough will look dry and there should still be bits of loose flour in the bowl. Do not overwork the dough!

3. **Knead.** Turn the dough out onto a lightly floured surface and use your hands and a bench scraper to gather it together, folding and kneading it over itself in as few motions as possible until it comes together in a craggy mass. There may still be some dry bits on the counter. Rub your hands together to remove and incorporate any excess dough, and dust in additional flour as needed to prevent sticking. Press the dough into a 4-inch square about 1 inch thick.

4. **Shape.** Follow the instructions in photos 2 through 4 to shape the biscuits. Smush the trimmed-off excess dough together to make a mini biscuit or discard it.

5. **Chill.** Transfer the biscuits to the prepared sheet pan, about 3 inches apart. Place the sheet pan in the freezer, uncovered, for 10 to 15 minutes.

6. **Bake.** Brush just the tops of the biscuits with egg wash and top each with a pinch of flaky salt or sparkling sugar. Bake until the biscuits are tall and golden brown on top, 16 to 18 minutes. Let them cool for at least 5 to 10 minutes before serving.

Recipe Note

To use buttermilk powder instead of buttermilk, add 11 grams (1 tablespoon) of buttermilk powder to the dry ingredients and use 90 grams (⅓ cup + 1 scant tablespoon) of whole milk instead of the liquid buttermilk.

Work quickly to pinch and flatten the pieces of butter with your fingers, rubbing the flour into them until they are roughly the size of a quarter

Use the bench scraper to divide the square into quarters. Move the bench scraper in an up and down cutting motion, do not slide the blade along the counter to cut the dough.

Stack the 4 quarters on top of each other, then press down to flatten the tower into a 1-inch-thick square again. Dust the top with flour and use the bench scraper to help keep the edges straight. Repeat stacking and smushing two more times, finishing by pressing the dough into a 5-inch square ½ to ¾ inch thick.

Before cutting the biscuits, use the bench scraper to trim as little as you can from each side of the final square, just enough so the edges are straight. (This releases the tension on the outer edges so the flaky layers are exposed, allowing the biscuits to rise evenly in the oven.)

MINI VANILLA BEAN SCONES

MAKES
6 SMALL SCONES

CHILL TIME:
30 MINUTES

BAKE TIME:
18 TO 20 MINUTES

DOUGH

120g (1 cup)
all-purpose flour

40g (3 tablespoons
+ 1 teaspoon) + 4g to
8g (1 to 2 teaspoons)
granulated sugar

2g (heaping ½ teaspoon)
Diamond Crystal
kosher salt

1g (¼ teaspoon)
baking powder

42g (3 tablespoons)
cold unsalted butter,
cut into ¼-inch cubes

10g (2 scant teaspoons)
vanilla bean paste

85g (generous ⅓ cup)
+ 32 grams (2 tablespoons)
heavy whipping cream
cold from the fridge

ICING

20g (3 tablespoons)
powdered sugar

3g (generous ½ teaspoon)
vanilla bean paste

7g to 10g (1¼ to
1¾ teaspoons)
heavy whipping cream

Starbucks, *Shmarbucks*, now you can make adorable petite vanilla bean scones in the comfort of your own kitchen. Rich heavy cream in the dough *and* brushed on top before baking makes these scones super moist and tender, and you can even use the extra cream in the mug of coffee you'll undoubtedly want to dunk them in. While vanilla extract will work if you don't have vanilla bean paste, I really do recommend using the paste (which has visible flecks of real vanilla bean in it) if you can for a more intense vanilla flavor!

1. **Prep.** Line a sheet pan with parchment paper and set aside.

2. **Mix.** In a medium bowl, whisk together the flour, 40g of the granulated sugar, the kosher salt, and baking powder. Add the cold cubed butter and use your fingers and thumbs to pinch and flatten the butter cubes, rubbing them into the flour until you have lots of flat shards of butter about the size of a dime (photo 1). Make a well in the center and add the vanilla and the 85g cold cream. Use a dough whisk or a fork to mix the dough until lots of large clumps form—it will look like lumpy wet sand. The dough might look quite dry and there should still be dry bits left in the bowl (photo 2)—that's okay.

3. **Knead.** Turn the dough out onto a clean surface and use your hands to gently knead and fold it over itself until all the dry bits are incorporated (photo 3). Do not overwork the dough. As soon as all the dry bits hold together, use your hands like you're shaping a snowball to pack the dough into a grapefruit-size ball.

4. **Shape.** Place the dough ball on the prepared sheet pan and use your hand to flatten it into a 4-inch disc about 1 inch thick. Use a bench scraper to cut the disc into 6 wedges (like a pizza). Separate the wedges about ½ inch apart on the sheet pan.

5. **Chill.** Place the sheet pan, uncovered, in the freezer for 30 minutes.

6. **Preheat.** While the scones chill, preheat the oven to 425°F.

7. **Bake.** Immediately before baking, brush the tops of the scones with the 32g cold cream and sprinkle each with a pinch of granulated sugar. Bake until the scones are light golden brown on top, 18 to 20 minutes. Let the scones cool completely on the sheet pan before icing, about 1 hour.

recipe continues

8. Ice. In a small bowl, whisk together the powdered sugar, vanilla bean paste, and 7g cream until the icing has a spreadable texture (add the remaining cream only if the icing is so thick you can't spread it). Use a spoon or table knife to spread the icing over the tops of the cooled scones. Let the icing sit for 10 to 15 minutes to form a crust before serving.

Work quickly to pinch and flatten the pieces of butter with your fingers, rubbing the flour into them until they are roughly the size of a dime.

After mixing the heavy cream into the dough, it will still seem quite dry—that's normal!

Gently knead with your hands just until the dough comes together. Finish by shaping the dough into a ball like you're packing a snowball.

Flatten the dough on the sheet pan, then cut into 6 wedges. Always cut in a clean up-and-down motion to preserve the layers of butter inside the dough.

ALL-PURPOSE ALL-BUTTER PIE DOUGH

MAKES 1 ROUND OF DOUGH

CHILL TIME: 1 HOUR TO 3 DAYS

70g (5 tablespoons) unsalted butter, *cold from the fridge*

80g (⅓ cup) cold water (you will not need all the water!)

A handful of ice cubes

20g (4 teaspoons) distilled white vinegar

120g (1 cup) all-purpose flour + more for dusting

2g (heaping ½ teaspoon) Diamond Crystal kosher salt

This buttery, flaky pie dough (pâte brisée) can be used to make all sorts of pastry creations! It's big enough for one galette (page 184), one oversized breakfast tart (page 187), one batch of fruit-filled pastries (page 191), or you can use it in your favorite pie or galette recipe. One batch of this dough works for an 8- to 9-inch single crust pie, a 6- to 7-inch double crust pie, or a 9- to 10-inch galette. And since there's no sugar in it, that means it can swing sweet or savory, depending on your filling of choice!

1. **Prep.** Cut the butter into ½-inch cubes and refrigerate until ready to use. In a liquid measuring cup, combine the water, ice cubes, and vinegar. Set the measuring cup in the fridge until it's time to use it.

2. **Mix.** In a medium bowl, whisk together the flour and salt. Add the cold butter cubes and toss to coat. Mix the dough following the instructions in photos 1 and 2 until the dough holds together. Using your hand for this step helps you feel how hydrated the dough actually is—it will look dry even when there's plenty of water in it.

3. **Knead.** Turn the dough out onto a clean surface and use your hands to gather it together, folding it over itself and kneading gently until the dry bits are incorporated. Dribble or spray a tiny bit more ice water onto any dry bits *only if needed* to help the dough come together. Do not overwork the dough! The dough will have time to finish hydrating as it rests, so resist adding more water unless absolutely necessary.

4. **Preshape.** If making a round pastry, shape the dough into a ball, then flatten it into a disc about 1 inch thick. If making square pastries, use your hands to shape the dough into a square, then use a bench scraper to trim the edges and press them evenly onto the top of the square. Flatten the square of dough until it is about 1½ inches thick.

5. **Chill.** Wrap the dough tightly in plastic wrap and refrigerate for 1 hour or up to 3 days before use. If refrigerated overnight or longer, leave the dough out at room temperature for 10 to 20 minutes prior to rolling. (Pie dough can be frozen for up to 3 months. Thaw it in the fridge overnight before using.)

recipe continues

Recipe Note

The acid from the vinegar makes the dough extra tender, but if you don't have it on hand, using ice water alone will work just fine.

Working quickly, press the cubes of butter between your fingers and thumbs, rubbing flour into them as you flatten the butter into large shards about the size of a quarter. Continue tossing the butter pieces in the flour as you flatten and rub them apart until the biggest pieces are the size of quarters and well coated in flour.

Drizzle a little more than half the ice water (38g to 40g—be sure you're not weighing ice) over the flour and use one hand to gently toss until the water is just absorbed. Add more water, 8g (1½ teaspoons) at a time, using your hand to toss the flour with the water before adding more. Repeat two or three more times, until you can squeeze the dough together and have it hold its shape. (There might still be some dry bits of flour and visible chunks of butter—that's okay.)

BUTTER

Apple Galette

MAKES ONE 9-INCH GALETTE

CHILL TIME: 10 MINUTES

BAKE TIME: 26 TO 28 MINUTES

A galette is a flat pie with a thin layer of filling tucked inside a rustic crust. Perfect if you're like me and think the biggest flaw in a traditional apple pie is too many apples, not enough crust (don't @ me if you disagree). If you're after a loaded apple galette, double the amount of filling. Don't skimp on the sparkling sugar; it adds a lovely sweetness to the crust.

I've given a range of sugar amounts for the filling because apples come in so many varieties. Use more sugar if you're using very tart apples, less for sweeter apples. Don't like apples? Pears or peaches work well here, too!

All-Purpose All-Butter Pie Dough (page 181), shaped into a round disc, *cold from the fridge*

1 large crisp apple, such as Honeycrisp, Granny Smith, Pink Lady, etc., *peeled or unpeeled, cored, and sliced into ⅛- to ¼-inch crescents*

12g to 18g (1 to 1½ tablespoons) granulated sugar

3g (1½ teaspoons) ground cinnamon

2g (½ teaspoon) vanilla extract

Pinch of ground cardamom, ground allspice, and/or ground ginger (optional)

Egg wash: 1 large egg, *beaten well*

1 to 2 teaspoons sparkling sugar

7g (1½ teaspoons) unsalted butter, cut into four ½-inch cubes

1. Preheat. Preheat the oven to 425°F. Line a sheet pan with parchment paper and set aside.

2. Make the filling. In a medium bowl, use tongs to gently toss the apple slices with the granulated sugar, cinnamon, vanilla, and any additional spices until the apples are well coated. Set aside.

3. Shape. On a lightly floured surface, roll out the chilled dough until it is 12 to 13 inches across and about ⅛ inch thick. It doesn't have to be a perfect round; the edges may be rough and cracked—that's okay. Periodically lift the dough off the counter and rotate or flip it over to prevent sticking. Dust the surface of the dough lightly with more flour as needed. Carefully lift the dough onto the prepared sheet pan.

4. Fill. Follow the instructions in photos 1 and 2 to add the apple filling and create the folded outer crust.

5. Chill. Place the sheet pan in the fridge, uncovered, for 10 minutes.

6. Top. Brush the edges of the crust generously with the egg wash, then sprinkle the crust generously with the sparkling sugar. Sprinkle the top of the apples lightly with sparkling sugar, too. Place the 4 cubes of butter spaced evenly across the pie filling.

7. Bake. Bake until the crust is golden brown, 26 to 28 minutes. Let the galette cool on the pan for 10 minutes before serving.

Arrange the apple slices in rings, starting 2 inches from the edge of the dough. Then do the center ring. Use any broken or leftover pieces of apple to fill in any gaps around the outer edge (they'll be hidden under the folded crust).

Fold the 2-inch bare edge of dough up and over the filling, pleating and creasing as needed, to create the outer crust.

OVERSIZED NUTELLA *POP~ULAR* TART

MAKES ONE 8-INCH PASTRY

CHILL TIME: 10 MINUTES

BAKE TIME: 22 TO 25 MINUTES

This pastry is what those classic rectangular breakfast pastries *wish* they could be when they grow up. The theme of this cookbook might be small-batch recipes, but my goal with this recipe was to make it as *big* as possible. It's a gloriously oversize hand pie made with buttery pie dough and stuffed with as much Nutella as possible, then topped with a rich chocolate icing and plenty of sprinkles. It's a lot simpler to make than it looks and will definitely impress your friends, *if* you choose to share it with them.

POP TART

All-Purpose All-Butter Pie Dough (page 181), shaped into a square, *cold from the fridge*

75g (¼ cup) Nutella

Egg wash:
1 large egg, *beaten well*

1 to 2 teaspoons sparkling sugar

ICING

30g (scant ¼ cup) powdered sugar

5g (heaping 1 tablespoon) natural unsweetened cocoa powder

¼ teaspoon vanilla extract

8g to 13g (2 scant teaspoons to 2½ teaspoons) whole milk

2 teaspoons sprinkles

1. **Preheat.** Preheat the oven to 425°F. Line a sheet pan with parchment paper and set aside.

2. **Cut.** Roll the dough out into a 12 by 8-inch rectangle about ⅛ inch thick. Use a metal ruler and a pizza wheel to trim the rough edges to form a rectangle with straight edges and sharp corners. Cut the dough in half crosswise to form two identical rectangles.

3. **Prep the filling.** Warm the Nutella in the microwave for 15 to 20 seconds, then stir well. Fill a piping bag with the warmed Nutella (a piping bag makes adding the filling SO much neater and easier, but if you don't have one, a mini offset spatula will work).

4. **Assemble.** Use a bench scraper to lift one sheet of dough onto the prepared sheet pan. Add the filling following the instructions in photo 1. Brush the bare outer edge of the dough with the egg wash, then carefully place the other rectangle of dough on top. (Save the rest of the egg wash for step 6!) Press the edges down gently with your fingers, taking care not to squish the Nutella out. Use a fork to crimp the edges all the way around, sealing the Nutella inside (photo 2).

5. **Chill.** Place the sheet pan in the fridge, uncovered, for 10 minutes.

recipe continues

6. Bake. Immediately before baking, use the pizza wheel to trim a tiny bit from each side of the tart so the edges are nice and straight, removing as little excess dough as possible. Brush the surface of the dough generously with egg wash, then use a fork to poke 8 to 10 sets of holes in the top (photo 3). Sprinkle the outer ¼ inch of the crust with sparkling sugar. Bake until the tart is golden brown, 22 to 25 minutes. Transfer the tart to a wire rack and let it cool completely.

7. Make the icing. In a small bowl, whisk together the powdered sugar and cocoa powder. Add the vanilla and 8g of milk and whisk until a glossy icing forms. When you lift the whisk out of the bowl the icing should drip off, leaving a "ribbon" visible on the surface of the icing in the bowl (photo 4).

8. Decorate. Dollop the icing in the middle of the tart and use a mini offset spatula or the back of a spoon to spread it out, leaving a ½-inch border around the edges. Top with sprinkles and let the finished tart rest until the icing forms a crust, 5 to 10 minutes.

Pipe or spread a rectangle of Nutella on the dough, leaving a ½-inch border around the outside. If you're piping, use a toothpick or a mini offset spatula to fill in any gaps.

If the dough sticks to the fork as you crimp the dough, gently place your fingers on either side of the tines to hold the dough in place. Wiggle the fork a bit as you pull it up to unstick the dough.

Poking holes in the top layer of dough allows steam to escape while the tart bakes so it doesn't burst open or leak in the oven.

If your icing doesn't form ribbons like this after the first addition of milk, tweak the ingredients. To thicken: add more powdered sugar, 10g (1 heaping tablespoon) at a time. To thin it out: add more milk, 2g (¼ teaspoon) at a time.

FRUIT PRESERVE PASTRIES, TWO WAYS

MAKES
4 PASTRIES

CHILL TIME:
20 MINUTES

BAKE TIME:
22 TO 26 MINUTES

It was so hard to choose just one way to shape these flaky fruit preserve–filled pastries, so I'm giving you two different shaping options: one that's super simple and another that's a little bit fancier. Pick the approach that works best for you! Try one, try them both, try something entirely different, it's your kitchen and you make the rules. If that's not proof of just how versatile my all-purpose pie dough can be, I don't know what is!

All-Purpose All-Butter Pie Dough (page 181), shaped into a square, *cold from the fridge*

2 to 4 tablespoons fruit preserves or jam (any flavor!)

Egg wash: 1 large egg, *beaten well*

1 to 2 teaspoons sparkling sugar

1. Preheat. Preheat the oven to 425°F. Line a sheet pan with parchment paper and set aside.

2. Shape. On a lightly floured surface, roll the chilled dough into a 10-inch square about ⅛ inch thick. Try to keep the edges as straight as possible. As you roll, periodically lift the dough off the counter and rotate or flip it to prevent sticking. Dust lightly with more flour only as needed. Cut the square of dough into 4 equal squares, then follow the instructions in the photos to shape the dough into triangle turnovers (page 192) or diamond pastries (page 193).

3. Chill. Place the shaped pastries on the prepared sheet pan, then place the pan in the fridge, uncovered, for 20 minutes.

4. Bake. Immediately before baking, brush the surface of the dough (not any exposed filling) with egg wash and sprinkle generously with sparkling sugar. Bake until golden brown and flaky, 22 to 26 minutes. Let the pastries cool on the pan for 5 minutes, then transfer them to a wire rack to cool completely before eating.

recipe continues

TRIANGLE TURNOVERS

Place 1 tablespoon of preserves about ¼ inch inside the rough-edged corner of each dough square.

Fold the square in half, bringing opposite corners together. Pinch the corner to seal.

Align the edges and crimp with a fork to seal. Use the fork to poke a set of holes in the top of the pastry to allow steam to escape.

DIAMOND PASTRIES

Use a pastry wheel or a bench scraper to trim any uneven edges so you can cut four 5-inch squares with clean, straight edges.

Dust the top of each piece of dough *very* lightly with flour, then fold it in half to make a triangle. Use a pastry wheel or a bench scraper to make two cuts along the short edges, about ½ inch in, but do NOT cut all the way to the point.

Unfold the triangle into a diamond shape with the joined points at the top and bottom. Brush the entire surface of the dough lightly with egg wash, then fold the ½-inch border from one side across the middle to meet the inside point on the opposite side. Line up the edges as needed. Repeat with the other side.

Spoon ½ tablespoon of preserves into the diamond shape in the middle of the pastry.

BEIGNETS

MAKES
6 BEIGNETS

RESTING TIME:
1½ HOURS

COOK TIME:
3 TO 4 MINUTES

I was first introduced to beignets at Café du Monde, arguably the beignet capital of the world, on a trip to New Orleans several years ago. It basically ruined me for all other beignets. They're light and pillowy, piled up under veritable mountains of powdered sugar that melts and clings to the freshly fried golden brown dough. Beignets are yeast-leavened, typically cut into squares, and often served with coffee or café au lait. Of course, I would never claim that my humble recipe is anywhere near as good as Café du Monde's, but if you're craving a bit of New Orleans sweetness, I can promise they'll hit the spot.

120g (1 cup) all-purpose flour + more for dusting

18g (1½ tablespoons) granulated sugar

3g (1 teaspoon) instant yeast

2g (heaping ½ teaspoon) Diamond Crystal kosher salt

30g (2 tablespoons) whole milk, *warmed* (90°F)

14g (1 tablespoon) unsalted butter, *melted*

1 large egg, *at room temperature*

¼ teaspoon vanilla extract

4 to 5 cups canola, vegetable, or peanut oil

2 to 4 tablespoons powdered sugar

1. Mix. In a medium bowl, whisk together the flour, granulated sugar, yeast, and salt. In a second bowl or a liquid measuring cup, whisk together the warm milk, melted butter, egg, and vanilla. Make a well in the center of the dry ingredients and pour in the wet ingredients. Use a dough whisk or a fork to mix until large clumps form, then use a bowl scraper or your hand to fold the dough over itself in the bowl until it comes together in a cohesive mixture with no dry bits.

2. First rest. Gather the dough together in a sticky ball in the bottom of the bowl, cover, and let it rest for 5 minutes.

3. Knead. Turn the dough out onto a well-floured surface. Knead with a light touch for about 1 minute, just until the dough smooths out. Don't worry if all the flour isn't incorporated—you want the dough to still feel a little loose and sticky.

4. Rise. Lightly grease the bowl with a thin film of oil. Tuck the dough into a loose ball and place in the greased bowl. Cover and let the dough rise at room temperature until it passes the Fingerprint Test (page 20), 1 to 1½ hours. (The dough won't double in size.)

5. Shape. Turn the dough out onto a lightly floured surface. Shape the beignets following the instructions in photos 1 and 2.

6. Second rest. Cover the rectangles with a clean kitchen towel and let them rest on the counter for 30 minutes.

7. Heat the oil. When there are 10 minutes left in the final rest, pour ½ to 1 inch of oil into a medium pot or sauté pan and heat the oil to 350°F over medium heat. Line a sheet pan with paper towels and place a wire rack inside.

8. Fry. Working in batches of 2 or 3, fry the beignets until they're deeply browned, 1 to 2 minutes per side (photo 3). The oil temperature will drop when you add the beignets, so adjust the heat as needed to maintain 350°F. Use a spider skimmer or slotted spoon to transfer the finished beignets to the wire rack. (They should have an internal temperature of at least 200°F, photo 4.) Dust the beignets generously with the powdered sugar and serve immediately.

Dust the top of the dough lightly with flour, then roll it into a 6-inch square that's about ½ inch thick. Tug on the corners gently and periodically press the edges of the dough against a bench scraper to encourage the square shape as you roll.

Use a bench scraper or a knife to divide the dough in half, then divide each half into thirds, so you have 6 rectangular pieces, each about 2 by 3 inches.

Fry the beignets until they're deeply browned, 1 to 2 minutes per side, adjusting the temperature of the burner to maintain the oil at 350°F. Take care not to puncture the beignets when you flip them, you don't want them to fill with oil! If they do, just make sure to let the oil drain out over the pot before transferring to the rack to cool.

Use an instant-read thermometer to make sure the beignets have reached an internal temperature of at least 200°F. If they need more cooking time, be sure to keep the thermometer hole on top.

IRISH SODA BREAD

MAKES
1 SMALL LOAF

BAKE TIME:
21 TO 23 MINUTES

Soda bread is super easy, super fast, and a great way to get a nice homemade bread on the table ASAP! It has a thick, crunchy crust and a tender, slightly crumbly interior. The name comes from the fact that it uses baking soda instead of yeast to rise—the baking soda reacts with acidic buttermilk to form bubbles inside the dough almost immediately. Cut your soda bread into thick slices and serve warm with salted butter and jam, or tear it into chunks and use it to soak up your favorite hearty stews.

120g (1 cup) all-purpose flour + more for dusting

3g (¾ teaspoon) sugar

3g (1 teaspoon) Diamond Crystal kosher salt

3g (½ teaspoon + ⅛ teaspoon) baking soda

40g (2 tablespoons + 2 teaspoons) buttermilk, *cold from the fridge*

14g (1 tablespoon) unsalted butter, *melted*

1 large egg, *cold from the fridge*

20g (2 tablespoons) dried currants (optional)

1. **Preheat.** Preheat the oven to 400°F. Line a sheet pan with parchment paper.

2. **Mix.** In a medium bowl, whisk together the flour, sugar, salt, and baking soda. Make a well in the center and add the buttermilk, melted butter, and egg. Use a dough whisk or a fork to vigorously whisk the liquids in the center until they're combined. Then continue mixing, gradually incorporating the dry ingredients from the sides just until the liquid is absorbed and large clumps have formed. Add the currants, if desired, and switch to a bowl scraper or your hand to fold the dough over itself a few times until it mostly comes together. It's okay if there are still some dry bits in the bowl.

3. **Knead.** Turn the dough out onto a lightly floured surface and knead with a light touch—just until the dry bits are incorporated. Do not overwork the dough.

4. **Shape.** Follow the instructions in photo 1 to shape the dough into a domed loaf.

5. **Bake.** Use a sharp knife to cut a ½-inch-deep X into the top of the loaf (photo 2). Bake until the soda bread is golden brown, 21 to 23 minutes. Let it cool on the pan for 15 minutes before serving.

Recipe Note

You can use buttermilk powder instead of buttermilk by adding 6g (2 teaspoons) of buttermilk powder to the dry ingredients and using whole milk instead of buttermilk.

Cup your hands around the dough, rotating and squeezing like you're shaping a snowball to form a round ball. Place the dough ball on the prepared sheet pan and cup your hands around it again, pinkies flush against the counter, pressing down slightly to flatten out the bottom, leaving a domed top.

Cut a ½-inch-deep X into the top of the loaf. If the dough is sticky and doesn't cut cleanly, you may need to dust the top with flour and retrace the cuts with your knife to clean up the X so the dough can expand properly in the oven.

SWEET LOAF~PAN CORNBREAD

MAKES
1 LOAF

RESTING TIME:
10 TO 20 MINUTES

BAKE TIME:
40 TO 45 MINUTES

This sweet cornbread loaf is made with a small can of creamed sweet corn. The corn kernels plus the yellow cornmeal provide that bright yellow color and amazing corn flavor, while the brown sugar and the olive oil make the cornbread extra moist and tender. I've written the recipe to bake in a single 9 by 5-inch or 8 by 4-inch loaf pan so you can cut it into thick slices, but you can also bake it as 6 standard-size muffins (decrease the bake time to 25 to 27 minutes).

Cooking spray

120g (1 cup)
all-purpose flour

90g (½ cup + 1 tablespoon)
medium-ground
yellow cornmeal

80g (6½ tablespoons)
brown sugar + 1 teaspoon
for topping

6g (2 teaspoons)
Diamond Crystal
kosher salt

4g (1 teaspoon)
baking powder

240g (one 8.5-ounce can)
cream-style sweet corn

1 large egg, *at room temperature*

24g (2 tablespoons)
olive oil

1. **Prep.** Preheat the oven to 350°F. Grease a loaf pan with cooking spray and set aside.

2. **Mix.** In a medium bowl, whisk together the flour, cornmeal, 80g brown sugar, the salt, and baking powder (use your hands to break up any large clumps of brown sugar). Make a well in the center and pour in the cream-style corn, egg, and olive oil. Use a dough whisk or a fork to break the egg yolk and whisk the liquid ingredients together in the center. Continue with a dough whisk or switch to a spatula, folding the wet ingredients into the dry just until everything is combined and no visible dry patches of flour remain—DO NOT OVERMIX! It's okay if the batter is lumpy, you just don't want any sneaky large pockets or streaks of flour hiding inside.

3. **Rest.** Pour the batter into the prepared loaf pan. Let rest, uncovered, for 10 to 20 minutes so the cornmeal hydrates and the baking powder activates.

4. **Bake.** Immediately before baking, sprinkle the remaining 1 teaspoon brown sugar over the top of the loaf. Bake until the center is set and the loaf is just barely browned around the edges, 40 to 45 minutes, or until it reaches an internal temperature of 200°F. A toothpick inserted into the center should come out clean. Let the cornbread cool in the pan on a wire rack for 20 minutes, then turn it out onto the rack to continue cooling for 10 to 15 minutes more. Serve warm.

ACKNOWLEDGMENTS

Writing a cookbook is truly a team effort, and this book would not exist without the help and support of so many people, starting with my husband, Jimmy, who guarded my time and energy while I was extremely pregnant and recipe testing, who took our newborn daughter on so many adventures out of the house so I could finish my manuscript after she was born, and who washed (I can't stress this enough) *so many dishes.* A huge thank-you also to my parents; my sister, Hannah, and her husband, John, as well as my in-laws, Margie and Doug; Kim and Adam, and their kids, Emma, Wyatt, and Connor, who dutifully taste-tested so many of my recipes throughout the development process. To Kristin Donnelly without whom my book proposal never would have gotten off the ground, and to my recipe testers, Afton Cyrus and Andrea Wawrzyn, who helped ensure every recipe works as written, I am so glad our paths crossed.

Shooting a cookbook postpartum was no easy feat and I feel so lucky to have had the most joyful photo shoot experience thanks to my amazing photography and crew: Linda Campos, Joy Howard, Karraline Streifel, Sāsha Coleman, Sophie Frazier, Laura Manning, and Kaylei McGaw. To Betsy Stromberg and Francesca Truman, thank you for making my first book so deliciously beautiful. I'm also eternally grateful to Erin Clarkson, Sam Garner, and Cynthia Christensen, who were instrumental sounding boards throughout this whole process. Finally, to my agent, Sally Ekus, and my editors, Molly Birnbaum and Kristin Sargianis, thank you for being as excited about this book as I am.

I also have to thank Liane Walker and Foodie Digital, Jonathan Zittrain, Carly Gillis, Evan Porter, Andrew Janjigian, Aubrey Gordon, Susan Reid, Sabrina Toppa, and everyone at Cambridge School of Culinary Arts (specifically my instructors Chef Jody O'Sullivan and Chef Sharon Donovan), and a huge thanks for the snuggles to my cats, Bones (RIP!) and Clementine.

To all the readers and fans of *The Practical Kitchen*—thank you. This book exists because you have liked, shared, commented, baked, and loved my recipes, and I am so lucky that I get to do this as a job because of you.

A very special thanks to my volunteer recipe testers: Alicia Hodson, Amy, Amy Tyszkiewicz, Amy Wolfe, Andrea, Angilique Falcon, Becky McDonald, Beth A, Beth Armstrong, Bonnie Danihelka, Cassie, Christine Robb, Debby Lowenstein, Dian McKelvey, Emily Padgett, Erica F, Erin Thiessen, Frances Morris, Frances Russo, Gwendolyn Downing, Heather, Heather F., Jackie, Jennifer Bodenhoefer, Jennifer Krause, Josephine Lyman, Judy Torchiana, Julie, Karen Baynton, Karen Schnee, Karine Hickey, Kate Law, Katie Baldwin, Kim Kalmanir, Laurie Boucher, LeAnne, Lesly, Lisa Milideo, Lucy Lambert, Margaret MacLellan, Martha Claugus, Meg Lally, Megan Georgette, Megan Milan, Megan Schwarz, Molly, Monique (EatinistBitch), Nic Meek-Whitehead, Pattie Homann, Rachel Battis, Rebecca Vann, Samantha F, Sandi Sawa Hazlewood, Sean Tibbitts, Summer Miller-Walfish, Valerie Bobb, Vicki, Vicki Johnson, and Viki Gerds.

INDEX

italics indicate photographs.

A

B

C

FOR MABEL,
THE BEST SMALL BATCH
I'VE EVER BAKED

TEN SPEED PRESS
An imprint of the Crown Publishing Group
A division of Penguin Random House LLC
1745 Broadway
New York, NY 10019
tenspeed.com
penguinrandomhouse.com

Text copyright © 2026 by Rebecca Eisenberg
Photographs copyright © 2026 by Linda Campos
Penguin Random House values and supports copyright. Copyright fuels creativity, encourages diverse voices, promotes free speech, and creates a vibrant culture. Thank you for buying an authorized edition of this book and for complying with copyright laws by not reproducing, scanning, or distributing any part of it in any form without permission. You are supporting writers and allowing Penguin Random House to continue to publish books for every reader. Please note that no part of this book may be used or reproduced in any manner for the purpose of training artificial intelligence technologies or systems.

TEN SPEED PRESS and the Ten Speed Press colophon are registered trademarks of Penguin Random House LLC.

Typefaces: Resistenza's Archivio, Linotype's Melior, and Monotype's Nolan Next.

Library of Congress Cataloging-in-Publication Data has been applied for.

ISBN 978-0-593-83772-6
Ebook ISBN 978-0-593-83773-3

Acquiring editor: Molly Birnbaum
Project editor: Kristin Sargianis
Production editor: Christine Tanigawa
Designer: Francesca Truman
Art director: Betsy Stromberg
Production designers: Mari Gill and Faith Hague
Production & Prepress color manager: Jessica Heim
Food stylist: Joy Howard | Food stylist assistants: Sāsha Coleman, Sophie Frazier, Laura Manning
Prop stylist: Kaylei McGaw / Anchor Artists | Prop stylist assistant: Lauren Gilgan / Anchor Artists
Photo assistant & Digitech: Karraline Streifel | Photo retoucher: Christopher Lee Donovan
Copy editor: Kate Slate | Proofreader: Rachel Holzman
Compositors: Nick Patton and Hannah Hunt
Indexer: Elizabeth Parson
Marketer: Chloe Aryeh

Manufactured in China

10 9 8 7 6 5 4 3 2 1

First Edition

The authorized representative in the EU for product safety and compliance is Penguin Random House Ireland, Morrison Chambers, 32 Nassau Street, Dublin D02 YH68, Ireland, https://eu-contact.penguin.ie.